URBAN TRAILS

TRAILS

PORTLAND

URBAN TRAILS

TRAILS

PORTLAND

Beaverton · Lake Oswego
Troutdale

ELI BOSCHETTO

MOUNTAINEERS
BOOKS

MOUNTAINEERS BOOKS is the publishing division of The Mountaineers, an organization founded in 1906 and dedicated to the exploration, preservation, and enjoyment of outdoor and wilderness areas.

1001 SW Klickitat Way, Suite 201, Seattle, WA 98134
800-553-4453, www.mountaineersbooks.org

Printed in China
Distributed in the United Kingdom by Cordee, www.cordee.co.uk
First edition, 2018

Copyeditor: Erin Cusick
Design: Jen Grable
Layout: Peggy Egerdahl
Cartographer: Pease Press Cartography

Cover photograph: *Magnolias at the Hoyt Arboretum (Hike 2)*
Frontispiece: *One of the many trails on Portland's Mount Tabor (Hike 21)*

All photographs by the author unless otherwise noted.

Library of Congress Cataloging-in-Publication Data
Names: Boschetto, Eli author.
Title: Urban trails. Portland : Beaverton, Lake Oswego, Troutdale / Eli Boschetto.
Other titles: Portland
Description: First edition. | Seattle, Washington : Mountaineers Books, [2018] | Includes index.
Identifiers: LCCN 2018010943 (print) | LCCN 2018005754 (ebook) | ISBN 9781680511222 (paperback) | ISBN 9781680511239 (ebook)
Subjects: LCSH: Hiking—Oregon—Portland Region—Guidebooks. | Walking—Oregon—Portland Region—Guidebooks. | Running—Oregon—Portland Region—Guidebooks. | Trails—Oregon—Portland Region—Guidebooks. |
   Outdoor recreation—Oregon—Portland Region—Guidebooks. | Portland (Ore.)—Guidebooks. | Portland Region (Ore.)—Guidebooks.
Classification: LCC GV199.42.O72 (print) | LCC GV199.42.O72 P6735 2018 (ebook) | DDC 796.5109795/49—dc23
LC record available at https://lccn.loc.gov/2018010943

ISBN (paperback): 978-1-68051-122-2
ISBN (ebook): 978-1-68051-123-9

CONTENTS

GETTING ACQUAINTED WITH PORTLAND'S PARKS

NORTH PORTLAND

FOREST PARK

PORTLAND WEST

PORTLAND EAST

LAKE OSWEGO

BEAVERTON

TROUTDALE

PORTLAND 40-MILE LOOP

Trail Locator Map

St. Helena

Ridgefield

5

Scappoose

30

6

Sauvie Island

5

Battle Ground

Columbia

Willamette

River

Vancouver

Ridgefield

14

205

WASHINGTON

OREGON

Camas

to Columbia River Gorge

7

FOREST PARK

13

8

North Portland

Portland International Airport

37

33

14

12

11

Willamette

River

Northeast Portland

84

East Portland

84

34

Troutdale

Sandy River

26

30

8

to Hillsboro

10

3

10 14

1 15

9 2

Down-town

19 20

18 PORTLAND

21

26

24

Gresham

35

16

17

Beaverton

217

5

23

22

Southeast Portland

36

205

Happy Valley

Boring

Hazeldale

31

Tigard

4

224

25

Clackamas

212

26

to Sandy

210

26

Milwaukie

99E

32

Tualatin

27

Lake Oswego

28

West Linn

29

Oregon City

205

Sherwood

99W

to Newburg

Wilsonville

Willamette River

Estacada

Clackamas River

Canby

213

99E

N

0   10 Mile

1 Hike location

5

Woodburn

TRAILS AT A GLANCE

Trail/Park	Distance	Walk	Hike	Run	Bike*	Kids	Dogs
GETTING ACQUAINTED WITH PORTLAND'S PARKS							
1. Portland Audubon Sanctuary	4.5 miles of paths and trails	•	•			•	
2. Hoyt Arboretum	12 miles of paths and trails	•	•	•		•	•
3. Tualatin Hills Nature Park	5 miles of paths and trails	•	•	•	•	•	
4. Tryon Creek State Natural Area	8 miles of paths and trails	•	•	•	•	•	•
NORTH PORTLAND							
5. Warrior Rock Lighthouse	6 miles roundtrip	•		•		•	•
6. Oak Island Nature Trail	2.7 miles roundtrip	•		•		•	•
7. Kelley Point Park	2.2 miles of trails	•		•	•	•	
8. Smith and Bybee Wetlands	1.7 miles roundtrip	•			•	•	
FOREST PARK							
9. Wildwood Trail and Leif Erikson Drive	41 miles of trails	•	•	•	•	•	•
10. Dogwood Loops	3.3 miles of trails		•	•		•	•
11. Maple Loops	8.5 miles of trails		•	•		•	•
12. Trillium Loops	4.6 miles of trails		•	•		•	•
13. Waterline Loops	5.1 miles of trails		•	•	•	•	•

*May be limited to specific trails

Trail/Park	Distance	Walk	Hike	Run	Bike*	Kids	Dogs
PORTLAND WEST							
14. Lower MacLeay Park: Balch Creek	2.2 miles roundtrip	•	•	•		•	•
15. Upper MacLeay Park: Pittock Hill	2.7 miles of trails		•	•		•	•
16. Marquam Nature Park: North Loop and Council Crest	3.8 miles of trails		•	•		•	•
17. Marquam Nature Park: South Loop	1.7 miles roundtrip	•	•	•		•	•
PORTLAND EAST							
18. Tom McCall Waterfront Park	4.4-mile loop	•		•	•	•	•
19. Lone Fir Cemetery	1.3 miles of paths	•				•	
20. Laurelhurst Park	2.2 miles of paths	•		•		•	•
21. Mount Tabor Park	12.5 miles of paths, trails, and roads	•	•	•	•	•	•
22. Crystal Springs Rhododendron Garden	2 miles of paths	•				•	•
23. Oaks Bottom Wildlife Refuge	2.8 miles roundtrip	•		•		•	
24. Powell Butte Nature Park	13.2 miles of paths and trails	•	•	•	•	•	
25. Mount Talbert Nature Park	3.9 miles of trails	•	•	•		•	

*May be limited to specific trails

Trail/Park	Distance	Walk	Hike	Run	Bike*	Kids	Dogs
LAKE OSWEGO							
26. Springbrook Park	2.1 miles of trails	•		•	•	•	•
27. Cooks Butte Park	2.5 miles of trails	•	•	•		•	•
28. Mary S. Young State Recreation Area	5.7 miles of paths and trails	•	•	•	•	•	•
29. Camassia Natural Area	1.1 miles of trails	•		•		•	
BEAVERTON							
30. Orenco Woods Nature Park	1.5 miles of paths and trails	•		•	•	•	•
31. Cooper Mountain Nature Park	3.8 miles of trails	•	•	•		•	
32. Tualatin River National Wildlife Refuge	4.5 miles of trails	•				•	
TROUTDALE							
33. Blue Lake Regional Park	3 miles of paths and trails	•		•	•	•	
34. Sandy River Delta	9.3 miles of trails	•	•	•	•	•	•
35. Oxbow Regional Park	12 miles of trails	•	•	•	•	•	
PORTLAND 40-MILE LOOP							
36. Springwater Corridor and Tideman Johnson Park	3 miles roundtrip	•		•	•	•	•
37. Columbia River Trail	11 miles of paths	•		•	•	•	•

*May be limited to specific trails

Stickwork sculptures at Orenco Woods (Hike 30)

INTRODUCTION

*Everybody needs beauty as well as bread, places to play in
and pray in, where nature may heal and cheer
and give strength to body and soul alike.*
—John Muir

This guide is intended to introduce you to Portland's thousands of acres of parks, gardens, urban forests, nature preserves, and open spaces—and inspire you to get out and explore them. Whether you're a native or recent transplant, a new family or active outdoorsperson, you will find a wealth of opportunity for getting a high-quality nature fix without traveling far. In locations throughout the city, in places big and small, you'll find miles of walking paths, hiking trails, and bike routes, all connecting the area's communities and showcasing and preserving the natural and cultural heritage of Portland's unique and special place in the Northwest.

When John Muir wrote the words above, he could have been channeling landscape architects Frederick and John Olmsted. Just a decade earlier, they shared a similar sentiment about the development of the city of Portland, then a barren landscape of clear-cut forest—hence one of its nicknames: "Stumptown." In planning the 1905 centennial of the Lewis and Clark Expedition, the Olmsteds were tasked with conceiving a grand plan for the creation of a network of parks as a way to beautify the city and provide natural spaces for the residents to relax and recreate. Their plan was not short-sighted as, in the end, they conceived a master park plan that anticipated the growth and needs of the city well into the future.

It is true that some people look upon such woods merely as a troublesome encumbrance standing in the way of more profitable use, but future generations will not feel so and will bless the men who were wise enough to get such woods preserved.

—John Olmsted

The plan started with a small forest reservation between the city center and Lake Oswego, what is now Tryon Creek State Natural Area. That quickly grew to more park and preserve locations that included the Willamette River, Columbia Slough, Ladd's Addition, Mount Tabor, and Sellwood. The jewel in Portland's crown, however, was to be Forest Park, about which Olmsted uttered the comment above. That sentiment was seconded in 1912 by fellow landscape architect Edward Bennett, though nearly forty years passed before Forest Park was finally dedicated as a public city park in 1948. The jewel was set. In the decades since, Portland and its neighboring communities have continued to prioritize the need for parks and green space as the area has grown and the population has increased.

Of course, when you ask locals what is most notable about Portland, the responses you're likely to get may range from food trucks and farmers markets to bike commuters and breweries, tattoos and tacos (yes, tacos!) to dogs and donuts, hipsters and hippies to music and marijuana (it's legal!). The rare few may suggest parks and peaks, forests and flowers, trees and trails. But the fact is that trees and green spaces are so integrated into Portland's culture and community that while they may go overlooked, they are nonetheless always appreciated and admired. And that attribute continues to earn Portland recognition as one of the best cities to live, according to *Money* magazine, along with the moniker "Silicon Forest," for its progressive, tech-savvy culture combined with environmental consciousness and an abundance of urban nature.

A forest in the city

> *Portland's parks, public places, natural areas, and recreational opportunities give life and beauty to our city. These essential assets connect people to place, self, and others. Portland's residents treasure and care for this legacy, building on the past to provide for future generations.*
>
> —Portland Parks and Recreation

Among the hundreds of parks and natural spaces around the Portland area, Forest Park gets the most recognition—and deservedly so—as America's largest urban forest with more than 80 miles of hiking trails and biking paths. Yet there's more than just forest to explore in and around the city. There are also plenty of opportunities for wandering the banks and wetlands of Portland's three major rivers, as well as hiking on volcanic buttes, strolling through community gardens, discovering historic sites, and walking urban footpaths. Added to that, you may observe some of the hundreds of species of birds and wildlife that reside in these areas, where you practically have an urban safari at your doorstep.

No car, no problem. A century ago, as part of the Olmsteds' original plan, public accessibility to parks was a priority. That strategy continues to exist. And with Portland being one of the most pedestrian-friendly cities in the United States, just about everything—including parks and trails—is within easy walking, biking, or busing distance. This makes it especially convenient to head out for morning coffee, take a hike or a ride, grab lunch, pick up groceries, then head home without ever having to get in a car—and this helps reduce Portland's greenhouse gas emissions, which is good for people and parks alike. Of course, you can drive as well—a few of the destinations in this book do require that, and most have parking areas and other amenities. Most of the trails in this guide can usually be reached from the central metro area in less than thirty minutes.

Best of all, the trails listed in this guide were selected to offer a variety of trail lengths and difficulties in order to appeal to all ages and abilities. You'll find everything from family-friendly parks with nature centers and barrier-free paths to long-distance routes and steep grinders for big workouts. Check out the trails nearest you, then go farther and explore more. Most locations even offer multiple trails, so you have even more to choose from. This ensures that you will not run out of local trails to roam for quite some time. Now turn the page, pick a trail, grab your shoes, and get outdoors.

HOW TO USE THIS GUIDE

THIS EASY-TO-USE GUIDE PROVIDES YOU with the information you need to get out and walk, hike, and bike around Portland's urban parks, preserves, and natural areas. It gives you detailed summaries of each location while leaving enough room for your own personal discovery. Every trail and path in this guide was personally hiked to ensure that the information, directions, and advice are accurate and up to date. However, conditions can and do change, so it's a good idea to call ahead or visit a park's website to check the status of a trail before you go.

THE ROUTES

This book includes thirty-seven routes, paths, or park trail systems, covering trails in and around the greater Portland metro area, including destinations in Forest Park, Sauvie Island, Sellwood, Beaverton, Tualatin, Lake Oswego, West Linn, Clackamas, Gresham, and Troutdale. Paved routes are typically designated as "paths," and unpaved routes as "trails." Each route begins with the park or trail name followed by a block of information detailing the following:

Distance. Here you will find the roundtrip mileage (unless otherwise noted) of the featured route. If the location is a park or preserve with multiple trails, this figure represents the total mileage of trails within the location. In this case, the description gives an overview of the location's trail system. The mileage measurements in this guide were gathered using a Garmin 62S GPS device and then calculated with CalTopo mapping software. There may be some slight variances between this information and other park or trail information, but it will be very close.

Elevation gain. For single trails or routes, this figure indicates the cumulative difference of the entire route. This is not just the difference between the high and low points on the trail but also for all other significant changes in elevation along the way. For destinations where multiple routes are given, as in a trail network within a park, the elevation gain applies only to the steepest trail on the route.

High point. The high point is the highest elevation of the trail or trail system described. Almost all of the trails in the book are at relatively low elevations and are accessible year-round.

Difficulty. This factor is based not only on length and elevation gain of a trail or trail system but also on the type of tread and surface area of the trail(s). Most of the trails in this book are easy to moderate for the average walker, hiker, or runner. Depending on your level of fitness, however, you may find the trails more or less difficult than described.

Fitness. This description denotes whether the trail is best for walkers, hikers, or runners. Generally, paved paths will be of more interest to walkers, runners, and persons with mobility challenges, while rough, hilly trails will appeal more to hikers. Of course you are free to walk, hike, or run any of the trails in this book (unless park regulations specifically indicate otherwise).

Family-friendly. Here you will find notes about a trail or park's suitability for children, and any cautions to be aware of such as cliffs, mountain bike use, and so on.

Dog-friendly. This indicates whether dogs are permitted on the trail or in the park, and what regulations apply. This will also indicate if there are off-leash areas at this location.

Bike-friendly. This notes whether bicycles are permitted on the trail or in the park, and if there are any restrictions to bike use.

Amenities. Look here for details about the location's amenities. This can include restrooms, benches, picnic tables, interpretive signs, viewpoints, shelters, visitor or learning centers, and more. Unless otherwise noted, restrooms and picnic areas are usually located at or near trailheads and visitor centers.

Management. The organization or administrative body that manages the trail or park is listed here. Contact details (website and phone number) are located in the appendix. Many park websites offer downloadable trail maps.

GPS. GPS coordinates are provided for the main trailhead to help you navigate to the trail. Coordinates are based on WGS84 degree measures.

Other. This section notes any fees or permits required, location hours (if limited), closures, and any other special concerns. This section may also indicate if the location hosts any special events, guided walks, workshops, or other opportunities. You'll find websites that are referred to in the appendix.

The route description then covers all the other information you'll need:

GETTING THERE. Each location includes a "Getting There" section that details the best means for getting to the trailheads, including driving directions and, where available, public transit options and bike routes. **Transit:** If the trailhead is served by TriMet public transportation (buses and MAX trains), this identifies the line and stop location. Visit www.trimet.org for transit maps, schedules, and fares. **Driving:** This provides directions to the trailhead via auto. These are generally from the nearest highway (e.g., I-5, I-84, I-205, I-405), major surface street, or neighborhood. **Bike:** If the trailhead is accessible by bike using designated bike routes or paths

LEGEND FOR TRAIL MAPS

🛣 5	Interstate Highway	🚹	Restroom/Outhouse
30	US Highway	Ⓐ	Picnic Area
4	State Highway	▪	Building/Landmark
	Surface Road	▲	Summit
	Unpaved Road		River/Stream
	Hiking Route		Lake
	Stairs		Wetland/Marsh
	Bike-Friendly Other Trail		Falls
	Other Trail		Park/Open Space
	Future Trail		Beach
Ⓢ	Start	] [	Bridge
Ⓢ	Alternative Start	⊷	Gate
Ⓟ	Parking	— · —	Powerline
+—+—+	Railroad	—◻—	MAX Line and Station

that vary from indicated driving directions, that route will be listed here.

EACH HIKE begins with an overview of the featured trail or park. Highlights include its setting and character, often with notes on the location's natural and cultural history.

GET MOVING describes the featured park or trail and what you might find on your walk, hike, or run; this section may note additional highlights, such as points of historical, natural, or cultural interest.

GO FARTHER gives suggestions for extending your outing by incorporating additional connecting trails and other nearby options.

RIDE IT offers suggestions for cyclists and mountain bikers to enjoy the trail also; some may suggest alternate directions or access points.

PERMITS, REGULATIONS, AND PARK FEES

Most of the trails and parks described in this book are managed by city and county parks departments. All but a few are free and do not require permits or fees. Destinations managed by Oregon State Parks or Metro may require a day-use fee. Each hike in this guide clearly states if a fee is charged or a pass is required. Regulations such as whether dogs are allowed, restricted hours, and closures for certain occasions are clearly indicated in each trail's information block.

ROAD AND TRAIL CONDITIONS

In general, trails change little year to year. But change can and does occur, and sometimes very quickly. A heavy storm can wash out sections of trail, and winter storms can blow trees down across trails. For some of the wilder destinations in this book, it is wise to check park websites or contact the appropriate land manager after a significant weather event to check on trail and road conditions.

It is an ongoing challenge to maintain many of the trails in Portland's parks and preserve areas. In addition to natural occurrences, parks are increasingly short-staffed and underfunded. There are several community volunteer groups that help by pitching in to take care of Portland's parks and trails. Consider joining one of these trail or conservation groups to help support your favorite park. You will find a list of these organizations in the appendix.

OUTDOORS ETHICS

A strong, positive outdoors ethic includes making sure you leave the trail (and park) in as good or even better condition than you found it. Get involved with groups and organizations that safeguard and advocate for land protection. Contact your local and state representatives and let them know how important protecting parks, public lands, and trails is to you.

LEAVE NO TRACE. All of us who recreate in Oregon's parks and natural areas have a moral obligation and responsibility to respect and protect these areas. The Leave No Trace Center for Outdoor Ethics (www.lnt.org) is an educational, nonpartisan nonprofit organization that was developed for responsible enjoyment and active stewardship of the outdoors. Their program helps educate outdoor enthusiasts regarding their recreational impacts and recommends techniques to prevent and minimize such impacts. While geared toward backcountry use, many Leave No Trace (LNT) principles are also sound advice for urban parks too, including: plan ahead, dispose of waste properly, and be considerate of other visitors.

PACK IT IN, PACK IT OUT. If you're going to be packing along snacks or a picnic to enjoy on your outing, please collect all your waste items to dispose of properly. Many parks provide waste and recycling containers to help keep parks clean. Carry an extra zip-top bag in your pack for collecting waste items to dispose of at home. You can even go one step further by picking up pieces of litter you find along your walks to help contribute to cleaner parks.

AVOID DISTURBING WILDLIFE. Observe birds and animals from a distance, and resist the urge to move closer to wildlife. This not only keeps you safer but prevents the animal from having to exert itself unnecessarily fleeing from you. If you're going to be visiting a park or preserve area where wildlife may be seen, take along binoculars or a telephoto lens for closer looks.

LOOK, DON'T TAKE. Follow the motto "Take only photos, leave only footprints" by leaving all natural things—including birds and animals, plants and flowers, and historic artifacts—as you find them for others to enjoy.

TRAIL ETIQUETTE

It is recommended that you be thoughtful not only to the environment surrounding our trails but to other trail users as well. Some of the trails in this book are open to mountain bikers and equestrians. When you encounter other trail users, whether they are hikers, runners, bicyclists, or equestrians, the only hard-and-fast rule is to follow common sense and exercise simple courtesy. Here are a few other things you can do when meeting other hikers to help make everyone's trip more enjoyable:

RIGHT-OF-WAY. When meeting bicyclists or horseback riders, those of us on foot should move off the trail. This is because hikers, walkers, and runners are more mobile and flexible than other users, making it easier for us to step off the trail.

ENCOUNTERING HORSES. When meeting horseback riders, step off the downhill side of the trail unless the terrain makes this difficult or dangerous. In that case, move to the uphill side of the trail, but crouch down a bit so you do not tower over the horses' heads. If you see a horse approaching, call out hello to make yourself visible and avoid startling the animal. If walking with a dog, keep it under control.

STAY ON TRAILS. Don't cut switchbacks, take shortcuts, or make new trails. This leads to erosion, unsightly trail degradation, and expensive trail repairs.

OBEY THE RULES. Many trails are closed to certain types of users, including dogs and mountain bikes. Some parks or trails are open only during specific hours or certain seasons. Be aware of any regulations that relate to the trail or park you are visiting.

WALKING WITH DOGS. If you hike with a dog, it is good practice—and common trail courtesy—to keep them on a leash at all times (unless in a designated off-leash area). Be aware that many trail users are not fond of, or may be afraid of, dogs—especially small children. Respect their right not to be approached by your pooch. Also, as a responsible dog owner, please pack out your dog's waste bags and do not leave them on the trailside to be collected (or forgotten) later. These are unsanitary and an eyesore to other visitors.

NEVER ROLL ROCKS OFF TRAILS. Gravity increases the impact of falling rocks exponentially, and you risk endangering fellow hikers or animals below you.

WATER AND GEAR

While most of the trails in this guide can be enjoyed without much preparation or gear, it is always a good idea to bring water and a few other supplies, even if you're just out for a quick walk or run. Carry a small backpack with a few snacks, sunglasses, and a rain jacket.

If you are heading out for a longer adventure—perhaps linking together several trails described in this guide—consider packing the **Ten Essentials**. Originated by The Mountaineers, the Ten Essentials are items intended to help outdoor recreationists prevent emergencies, respond positively should one occur, and safely spend an unplanned night outdoors should the need arise. Use this list as a guide and tailor it to the needs of your outing.

1. **NAVIGATION.** Download or pick up a map of the area you plan to visit and know how to read it. A cellphone or GPS unit are good to have along too.
2. **HEADLAMP.** If your hike runs late and you're caught out after dark, you'll be glad to have a headlamp or flashlight to help find your way back to the trailhead. Don't forget spare batteries.
3. **SUN PROTECTION.** Always carry sunscreen, rated at least SPF 30, and sunglasses, and wear sun-protective clothing—even on cloudy and rainy days. If the clouds break, you'll be glad for the extra coverage—especially if you're hiking out in the open or near water.
4. **FIRST AID.** At the very least, carry a small kit that contains bandages, blister prevention supplies, tweezers, pain relievers, antiseptic, and perhaps a small manual. If you have allergies (e.g., pollen or bees), you may also want to carry antihistamine tablets or an EpiPen. For longer outings, consider adding gauze, tape, scissors, anti-inflammatory

and anti-diarrheal tablets, and topical antibiotics. Don't forget any important personal prescriptions.

5. **KNIFE**. A pocketknife or multitool can come in handy, as can basic repair items such as duct tape, safety pins, and a small tube of superglue.

6. **FIRE**. Being forced to spend the night out is not likely on these trails, but a campfire could provide welcome warmth in an emergency. Carry at least one butane lighter (or waterproof matches in a zip-top bag) and fire-starter, such as chemical heat tabs, cotton balls or dryer lint soaked in petroleum jelly, or commercially prepared firestarter.

7. **SHELTER**. This can be as simple as a garbage bag or a rain poncho. There are also lightweight tarps and bivvy sacks you can carry that can double as picnic blankets.

8. **EXTRA FOOD**. Pack along a bag of trail mix, sports bars, or energy snacks for emergency pick-me-ups. For shorter trips, a one-day supply is reasonable; for longer outings, carry a little extra.

9. **EXTRA WATER**. Bring enough water to stay hydrated for the length of the trail you visit. For longer treks, consider carrying a water filter or purification method.

10. **EXTRA CLOTHES**. Weather and temperature can change quickly, so it's always advisable to carry an extra insulating layer (e.g., fleece or sweater) and raingear. Pack additional layers needed to survive the night in the worst conditions that your party may realistically encounter.

WILDLIFE

Oregon's parks are home to a variety of birds, mammals, and reptiles. The majority of these are small, scurrying critters—squirrels, chipmunks, and the like—gathering food and going about their daily routines for survival. A smaller number of residents are larger animals—beavers and deer, for example—doing the same and are typically docile. An even smaller number of large animals—coyotes, black bears, cougars—are also present, and while they are rarely seen, it's good to know how to respond to an encounter.

Bears are rarely aggressive and want little to do with humans. They will usually flee an area before you even know they are there. If you spot a bear, keep a safe distance and remain calm. Do not look a bear in the eyes as they perceive this as a challenge. Speak in a soft tone and back away slowly. The bear may bluff-charge, but do not run. If a bear acts aggressively, shout loudly and throw rocks and sticks; if it does attack, fight back using your fists, rocks, sticks, or trekking poles.

Cougar and coyote encounters are extremely rare, but they do occasionally occur in parks and preserves on the urban fringe. Minimize contact by not hiking or running alone and by avoiding carrion. If you do encounter a cougar or coyote, remember that they look for prey that can't or won't fight back. Do not run, but stand your ground and face the animal. Wave your arms, trekking poles, or a jacket over your head to appear bigger, and maintain eye contact. If you have children or small dogs with you, pick them up and back away slowly if you can do so safely. Do not take your eyes off the animal. If

A NOTE ABOUT SAFETY

Safety is an important concern in all outdoor activities. No guidebook can alert you to every hazard or anticipate the limitations of every reader. Therefore, the descriptions of roads, trails, routes, and natural features in this book are not representations that a particular place or excursion will be safe for your party. When you follow any of the routes described in this book, you assume responsibility for your own safety. Under normal conditions, such excursions require the usual attention to traffic, road and trail conditions, weather, terrain, the capabilities of your party, and other factors. Keeping informed on current conditions and exercising common sense are the keys to a safe, enjoyable outing.

—Mountaineers Books

the animal attacks, throw things at it, whack it with your trek-king pole, and, if necessary, fight back aggressively.

HUNTING

A few of the destinations in this book (e.g., on Sauvie Island) are open to bird hunting. Season dates vary, but generally the Oregon bird-hunting season takes place from fall to midwinter. While using trails in areas frequented by hunters, make yourself visible by wearing bright colors. If hiking with a dog, keep it leashed and put it in a bright-colored jacket too.

TRAILHEAD CONCERNS

Portland's parks and trails are generally safe places. Common sense and vigilance, however, are still suggested. This is true for all trail users, but particularly for solo walkers and hikers. Always let someone know when and where you're going, and stay aware of your surroundings at all times.

Unfortunately, car break-ins are a fairly common occurrence at some of our parks and trailheads. Do not leave anything—especially anything of value—in plain sight in your vehicle while out on the trail. A duffel bag on the back seat may contain dirty T-shirts, but a thief may think there's a laptop in it.

If you arrive at a trailhead and someone looks suspicious, don't discount your intuition. If something doesn't feel right, it probably isn't. Take action by leaving the place or situation promptly. If the person behaves inappropriately or aggressively, take notice of their appearance and their vehicle's make and license plate, and report the behavior to the authorities.

Despite these warnings, there is no need to be paranoid. The majority of trail users are just like you—out for exercise and to enjoy nature and the outdoors. Just use a little common sense while you're out and about.

Next page: *Discover giants in the Hoyt Arboretum's redwood and sequoia grove (Hike 2).*

GETTING ACQUAINTED WITH PORTLAND'S PARKS

If you're new to the Portland area, the Pacific Northwest, or just beginning to venture outdoors, then a visit to one of Portland's nature sanctuaries or interpretive parks should be one of your first outings. The following areas—conveniently located near the city center and communities west and south—are great entry-level experiences to help you get acquainted with the Pacific Northwest's flora, fauna, geology, and topography. Each location offers a visitor center with helpful staff, libraries, bookstores, nature guides, and easy walking paths suitable for all ages and abilities.

If you can, try taking an interpretive walk with a naturalist. They will point out small and interesting details, such as the way trees grow, how mosses form, and why rocks may be in the locations they are. They may also share Native American legends or historical accounts about certain areas. Some locations even have nature activities for kids. Once you've learned to identify Douglas firs and trilliums, vine maples and thimbleberries, you'll be ready to venture out into more of Portland's parks with the confidence that you'll know what you're seeing, and why you're seeing it.

1

Portland Audubon Sanctuary

DISTANCE:	4.5 miles of paths and trails
ELEVATION GAIN:	Up to 340 feet
HIGH POINT:	590 feet
DIFFICULTY:	Easy to moderate
FITNESS:	Walkers, hikers, some barrier-free
FAMILY-FRIENDLY:	Suitable for all ages
DOG-FRIENDLY:	Not permitted
BIKE-FRIENDLY:	Not permitted
AMENITIES:	Nature Store, Wildlife Care Center, restrooms, parking, interpretive info
MANAGEMENT:	Audubon Society of Portland
GPS:	N 45° 31.590', W 122° 43.818'
OTHER:	Trail hours sunrise to sunset; Nature Store hours 10:00 AM to 6:00 PM Monday–Saturday, 10:00 AM to 5:00 PM Sunday. The sanctuary provides a variety of kids camps and youth, adult, and school programs. Visit the Audubon Society website for more info.

GETTING THERE

Transit: TriMet bus 18 stops at the corner of NW Cornell Road and NW Westover Road. Walk 1 mile west on Cornell to the Audubon Sanctuary.

Driving: From Portland's Pearl District, drive west on NW Lovejoy Street approximately 1 mile. Veer right (northwest) at the fork onto NW Cornell Road. Proceed 1.5 miles to the Audubon Sanctuary Nature Store; parking is available on both sides of street.

Located near the east end of Forest Park, just minutes from downtown, the Portland Audubon Sanctuary is a 150-acre outdoor classroom that introduces visitors to the plants, forests, and wildlife typically found in Oregon's wetter western woodlands. When you arrive, stop in at the Nature Store to pick up a trail map and nature guide (or download and print before you go), then pay a visit to the Wildlife Care Center where sanctuary staff help rehabilitate wild birds, mammals, and amphibians who may have become injured or abandoned.

When you're ready to explore, start with the thirty-acre main sanctuary area situated in a deep ravine. A little more than a mile of trails and walking paths roam the banks of Balch Creek and the forested slopes above, which include a rare grove of old-growth Douglas fir and an even more rare giant sequoia. Kids of all ages will enjoy looking for frogs, turtles, and newts in the still-water pond, and birders can bring their binocs and try to spy some of the more than forty local

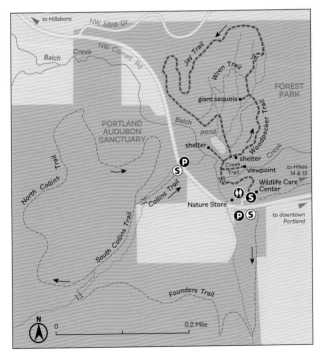

North Collins Trail

species, including jays, chickadees, nuthatches, towhees, bushtits, thrush, doves, hawks, and owls.

GET MOVING

Begin your 1-mile stroll at the Wildlife Care Center by descending into the ravine on a paved grade to a bridge over Balch Creek. Look for small tags along the trailside to help you identify the flowers and shrubs. Across the bridge, two short paths branch off to the right and left. To the right (east), the Creek Trail leads to a viewpoint where Balch Creek cascades through a narrow, rocky chute; to the left (west), the path leads to a shelter next to the still-water pond. Once you've checked out the river bottom features, veer right on the Woodpecker Trail to begin the main 0.9-mile loop. The route starts by climbing a small bluff to a shelter and viewing platform before turning upland into the forest. The way forward meanders easily among rhododendron, sword fern, and Oregon grape; mixed conifers and vine maple filter the sunlight overhead.

At the next junction, veer right (north) onto the Jay Trail, then descend left (west) to the sanctuary's towering giant sequoia. Crane your neck for an up-close look, and notice how rough and thick the orange-hued bark is compared to the nearby firs and cedars. Continue following the Jay Trail up a lush drainage (passing the Wren Trail cutoff), cross a bridge over a seasonal creek, then loop around the top of the sanctuary property. The way then starts a shallow descent, with salmonberry and thimbleberry along the trailside, and makes a wide hook out toward the roadway; look for pink sweet pea and yellow Saint-John's-wort blooming in the shrubby clearings. Close the loop by proceeding through a wooded wetland basin to meet the main trail back near the pond.

GO FARTHER

For a walk on the wilder side, find the Founders trailhead near the maintenance building on the south side of NW Cornell Road. Here, you can add up to 1.4 miles of heartier hiking on a high wooded slope. Proceed uphill on a moderate grade into a verdant drainage canyon. Where the canyon narrows, the path crosses a creek bed and begins a contouring ascent of the next slope. Near where the trail crests, look for the unusual big-leaf maple that appears to have eight separate trees growing out of a single massive trunk. Cross another creek and meet the junction for the South Collins Trail at 0.6 mile. If you're ready to head back, turn right (east) and head 0.2 mile down to the road. If you want to finish the full loop, turn left (west) onto the North Collins Trail and continue meandering through a grove of cottonwoods, then down a couple of wooded boardwalks, before hooking around the hillside. Descend into the drainage to meet the Collins Trail and turn left (east) to exit to NW Cornell Road. Walk the roadway southeast back to the Audubon Sanctuary.

2   Hoyt Arboretum

DISTANCE:	12 miles of paths and trails
ELEVATION GAIN:	Up to 380 feet
HIGH POINT:	860 feet
DIFFICULTY:	Easy to moderate
FITNESS:	Walkers, hikers, runners, some barrier-free
FAMILY-FRIENDLY:	Suitable for all ages; kid-friendly park activity map
DOG-FRIENDLY:	Leashed
BIKE-FRIENDLY:	Not permitted
AMENITIES:	Parking, restrooms, visitor center, picnic areas, interpretive walks and info, viewpoints
MANAGEMENT:	Portland Parks and Recreation
GPS:	N 45° 30.942', W 122° 42.954'
OTHER:	Park hours 5:00 AM to 9:30 PM; visitor center hours 9:00 AM to 4:00 PM Monday–Friday, 11:00 AM to 3:00 PM Saturday–Sunday. Arboretum staff and volunteers host a variety of guided walks, interpretive tours, nature classes, and maintenance opportunities for all ages. Visit the arboretum website for more info and a calendar of events.

GETTING THERE

Transit: From Portland, Beaverton, or Gresham, ride the MAX Blue Line to the Washington Park station. Find the arboretum south trailhead near the Vietnam Memorial, or ride the free Washington Park shuttle to the arboretum visitor center.

Driving: From I-405 in downtown Portland, take US Highway 26 west for approximately 1.5 miles. Take exit 72 for the Zoo and Forestry Center. Veer right onto SW Knights Boulevard and continue 0.8 mile into Washington Park, following signs for Hoyt Arboretum. Turn right onto SW Fairview Boulevard and proceed 0.1 mile to the arboretum parking area and visitor center.

Bike: Use transit to Washington Park, then ride using driving directions to the visitor center.

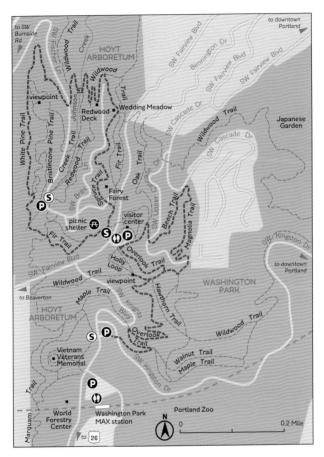

Whether you have an hour or a whole day, there's an outdoor amble waiting for you at the Hoyt Arboretum. Founded in 1928 as a living museum for the recreation and education of Portland's residents, the arboretum showcases more than two thousand species of trees and plants from around the world. Each significant species displays a small identification plaque to help you become acquainted with Northwest flora. Many

VIETNAM VETERANS OF OREGON MEMORIAL IN WASHINGTON PARK

Portland's Vietnam Veterans Memorial park

Inspired by Washington DC's Vietnam Veterans Memorial, Portland's Vietnam Veterans Memorial was dedicated in 1987 and is located on a pleasant grassy hillside between the World Forestry Center and the Hoyt Arboretum. The memorial consists of a partially paved, 0.2-mile spiraling walkway that showcases a series of memorial walls listing each Oregon resident who perished in the war by year. Each wall gives brief reflective accounts of the progression of the war through the years, in addition to concurrent events happening around Oregon, from the tragic to the trivial.

of these species are what you're likely to see in areas ranging from Portland's regional parks and wetlands to Oregon's Cascade Range and beyond. It starts with your first step.

From the arboretum's visitor center, you have 12 miles of paths and trails at your wandering whim. With each trail showcasing a different variety of plant or tree grouping, you can choose which you want to learn about and identify. Wander among deciduous maples, oaks, beeches, and walnuts, or observe evergreen redwoods, pines, firs, and spruces; in springtime, wander among flowering magnolias and dogwoods, or in fall, come and peep at the changing leaf colors. Grab a map before you set out, and follow your own path. Regardless of which trail you choose, you're bound to come away having learned a few things about the forest that you never knew.

GET MOVING

For a quick outdoor fix, or if you have little ones in tow, make a 0.7-mile loop out of the Magnolia and Beech Trails. This one is best in spring when the magnolia trees are brimming with big pink and white flowers. Start at the south end of the parking lot and make an easy ascent east on the Overlook Trail. When you reach the junction at the top, first veer right (west) on the Wildwood Trail into the clear for a nice view over open, grassy hillsides pocked with maple and ash trees; you may also spy the top of Council Crest (Hike 16) to the south. Turn back (east) and walk the Wildwood Trail for just a few paces to the Magnolia Trail; turn left (east) and descend into a fairy-tale-like garden and begin admiring. If the magnolias aren't blooming, look for clusters of pink creeping bellflower. Where the Magnolia Trail ends, veer left (west) onto the Beech Trail and begin an easy ascent under shady woods back to your starting point.

For more mileage, explore the arboretum's conifer groves by linking up portions of the Fir, Spruce, Wildwood, and White Pine Trails on a gently meandering 1.4-mile loop. Along the way, you'll encounter both native woods and rare exotic species, including dawn redwoods, Japanese larches, bristle-cone pines, ginkgoes, and Alaska yellow cedars. To begin, cross the road in front of the visitor center to the picnic shelter and turn right (north) onto the Fir Trail, then left (northwest)

Discover the trees, shrubs, and flowers of the Northwest at the Hoyt Arboretum.

onto the Spruce Trail. The path descends through the Fairy Forest (kids of all ages will love this) and past a giant Douglas fir that reveals what happens when trees are struck by lightning. Proceed past the Wedding Meadow, and when you reach the end of the line, turn left (south) onto the Wildwood Trail.

Before switchbacking all the way down, pause for a moment at the Redwood Deck. Here, you can admire a grove of skyscraping sequoias and coast redwoods that were planted in the 1930s. Still in their infancy, these trees could live up to two thousand years. Continue down the Wildwood, past the Creek Trail and over a bridge, and turn left (south) onto a connector spur to SW Fischer Lane. Cross the road and make an easy ascent northwest on the White Pine Trail; the route soon makes a U-turn and starts heading south along the arboretum's boundary. Continue on this path to a junction marked "private trail" and veer right (west) a few paces uphill to admire the arboretum's oldest Douglas fir. Crane your neck skyward for a look into its high canopy. When you meet the Fir Trail again, veer right (south) and follow the path back around to your starting point.

GO FARTHER

There are many more trails and trees to discover in the Hoyt Arboretum. These trail recommendations are just a starting point. Use your trail map to add on to either of the loops mentioned above, or explore other parts of the park. On the

HOYT ARBORETUM TRAIL CHECKLIST

See how many visits it takes for you to check off all fifteen trails in the arboretum.

❏ Beech Trail
❏ Bristlecone Pine Trail
❏ Creek Trail
❏ Fir Trail
❏ Hawthorn Trail
❏ Holly Loop
❏ Magnolia Trail
❏ Maple Trail

❏ Oak Trail
❏ Overlook Trail
❏ Redwood Trail
❏ Spruce Trail
❏ Walnut Trail
❏ White Pine Trail
❏ Wildwood Trail

Creek Trail, you can see the massive exposed root system of a giant western hemlock perched on the slope above the creek; on the Overlook Trail—particularly colorful in the fall—you can see a variety of unique deciduous trees, including maples, sumac, smoke trees, and birch bark cherries. Regardless of whether you explore short or long, near or far, you're bound to discover new things with each walk in these woods.

3 Tualatin Hills Nature Park

DISTANCE:	5 miles of paths and trails
ELEVATION GAIN:	Up to 90 feet
HIGH POINT:	195 feet
DIFFICULTY:	Easy
FITNESS:	Walkers, hikers, runners, cyclists, some barrier-free
FAMILY-FRIENDLY:	Suitable for all ages; be aware of poison oak
DOG-FRIENDLY:	Not permitted
BIKE-FRIENDLY:	Paved paths only
AMENITIES:	Parking, nature center, restrooms, interpretive info, benches
MANAGEMENT:	Tualatin Hills Parks and Recreation
GPS:	N 45° 29.892', W 122° 50.310'
OTHER:	Park hours sunrise to sunset; nature center hours 8:30 AM to 5:00 PM Monday–Friday, 9:00 AM to 5:00 PM Saturday and Sunday; closed holidays. The park's nature center hosts year-round interpretive walks and environmental education programs for kids and adults. Visit the nature center website for more info and a calendar of events.

GETTING THERE

Transit: Ride the MAX Blue Line west to Merlo Road Station at SW Merlo Road and SW 158th Avenue. Walk the short path from the MAX station right into the park.

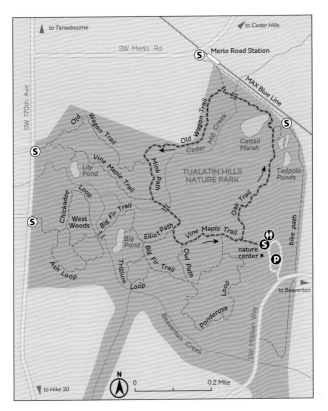

Driving: From downtown Portland, drive US Highway 26 west toward Beaverton for approximately 6 miles. Take exit 67 for SW Murray Boulevard; turn left (south) and continue 2.1 miles to SW Millikan Way. Turn right (west) and proceed for 0.6 mile to the park entrance on the right.

Bike: Ride the Westside Regional Trail to the park entrance at SW Millikan Way.

Nestled in the heart of Beaverton, among suburban housing developments, strip malls, industrial buildings, and the sprawling Nike campus, the Tualatin Hills Nature Park comprises 222 acres of protected wetlands, streams, and ponds amid pine, oak, maple, fir, and cedar. Within the park, 5 miles of looping, winding paths and trails provide short and long walking options for exploring the preserve. Interpretive signs along many of the routes provide information about the sights, including local plants and wildlife, making this a great outdoor classroom for getting acquainted with the Pacific Northwest's natural features.

Before getting started, visit the nature center and pick up a trail map and other brochures to help you identify the park's plants and wildflowers. There are also hands-on exhibits for kids, a reference library, and a small store that offers a selection of books and nature guides. Armed with your reference resources, hit the trails and connect one, two, three, or more of the park loops and discover what lies hidden in Beaverton's own backyard. As you're walking, keep your eyes peeled for a variety of songbirds, raptors, beavers, deer, and small scurrying critters.

GET MOVING

For an introduction to the nature park, or with little ones in tow, set out on a 1.5-mile stroll on wide, flat paths that explore the park's northern wetlands and Cedar Mill Creek. From the nature center, head out on the Vine Maple Trail. At the first junction, turn right (north) on the Oak Trail. The path meanders under a canopy of ponderosa pine and Oregon white oak amid ocean spray, blackcap, and corn lily. A sign warns that poison oak is abundant in the area—a good reason to stay on the trails. In springtime, trillium and violets are usually profuse along the trailside. Around the 0.5-mile mark, a short side trail branches right (east) to a viewpoint overlooking the small Tadpole Ponds; try to spot one of Oregon's rare red-legged frogs here.

At the next large junction, veer left (west) to stay on the Oak Trail. The path proceeds over a boardwalk at the edge of Cattail Marsh. Here, you may observe a variety of waterfowl, including ducks, geese, and herons. Scan the trees in this area for songbirds and great horned owls. The way then continues over a series of planked boardwalks over the marshes around Cedar Mill Creek, where more birds may be spied. At the next

Douglas firs on the Oak Trail

junction, at 0.75 mile, the way right (north) proceeds to the Merlo Road MAX station; turn left (west) and continue on the Old Wagon Trail. The path now skirts the northern boundary of the park, where interpretive signs illustrate how the park's bioswale protects local plants and animals.

The next junction comes at 1.1 miles. Here, the Old Wagon Trail continues right (west) and the Mink Path veers left (south). For this loop, turn left on the Mink Path for a short stretch to return to the Vine Maple Trail. (For a longer option, see Go Farther.) Turn left again and proceed over the large bridge that spans Cedar Mill Creek; scan the stream banks for rough-skinned newts. Now on the return leg, continue east on the Vine Maple Trail and meander under mossy trees with dangling licorice ferns, bypassing all side trails, and return to the nature center.

GO FARTHER

Create up to a 4.25-mile multi-loop tour of the park by combining any of the park's other trails with the loop above. Add a 0.75-mile extension to the loop by bypassing the Mink Path cutoff and continuing on the Old Wagon Trail. Proceed through reed grass and salmonberry to the upper junction with the Vine Maple Trail, then turn left (south) to head back to the nature center. On the way, take the short side trail to the Lily Pond and scan for some of the park's local residents. For more of a hike than a walk, veer southwest on the Elliot Path to the Big Fir Trail for a 1-mile lollipop loop through the park's West Woods, the oldest forested section, where tall Douglas firs and western red cedars provide homes for woodpeckers, wrens, and nuthatches above the banks of Beaverton Creek. Walk this loop in either direction. For wildflowers, explore the 0.2-mile Trillium Loop and the 0.5-mile Ponderosa Loop, where Oregon ash, trillium, salal, snowberry, and Oregon grape dominate the area. All connect with the Vine Maple Trail for mixing and matching loops at will.

4 Tryon Creek State Natural Area

DISTANCE:	8 miles of paths and trails
ELEVATION GAIN:	Up to 590 feet
HIGH POINT:	440 feet
DIFFICULTY:	Easy to moderate
FITNESS:	Walkers, hikers, runners, equestrians, cyclists, some barrier-free
FAMILY-FRIENDLY:	Suitable for all ages; some high bridges
DOG-FRIENDLY:	Leashed
BIKE-FRIENDLY:	Paved bike path only
AMENITIES:	Parking, nature center, restrooms, interpretive signs, picnic tables
MANAGEMENT:	Oregon State Parks
GPS:	N 45° 26.478', W 122° 40.536'
OTHER:	Park hours 7:00 AM to sunset; nature center hours 9:00 AM to 4:00 PM. The Friends of Tryon Creek offers interpretive walks, kids camps, adult education, and volunteer maintenance parties. Visit their website for more info and a calendar of events.

GETTING THERE

Transit: TriMet bus 39 stops on SW Terwilliger Boulevard near the north end of the park; walk 0.3 mile south to connect with the paved bike path and the park's north trailhead. TriMet buses 35 and 36 make stops near the south end of the park on SW Riverside Drive and N. State Street, both near SW Terwilliger Boulevard. From either, walk approximately 1 mile to Terwilliger, then north to connect with the paved bike path and on to the park's south trailhead.

Driving: From I-5, north or south, take exit 297 for SW Terwilliger Boulevard. Drive south on Terwilliger for 2.5 miles to the park entrance.

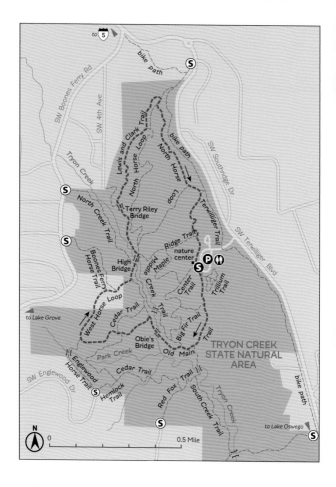

Bike: Use the paved bike path along SW Terwilliger Boulevard to the park entrance.

Just a short distance south of central Portland, tucked neatly into a lush, wooded canyon, Tryon Creek State Natural Area is a delightful destination for family outings, dog walking, or just taking a stroll through pretty woods. With more than 8 miles of easy to moderate walking paths and hiking trails, you can spend anywhere from a few minutes to a few hours roaming under shady Douglas firs and western red cedars while admiring an abundance of native shrubs and wildflowers around the park's namesake waterway. Before setting out, drop into the park's nature center and pick up a free park map and nature guide to help you find your way around the park's eighteen trails. These will also help you identify some of the flora and fauna you may observe on your outing.

GET MOVING

There are countless ways to explore Tryon Creek park. This description gives you just one option for hiking a 2.8-mile loop around the park's central area. If you want more, you can always add side trails or additional loops; less, just cut a few corners. Start at the nature center and head south on the Old

HIKE FOR YOUR HEALTH

With life's ever-increasing demands on our time and attention, a walk in the park is just what you need. According to Julie Corliss of *Harvard Health Publishing*, health and wellness studies have found that taking a walk in nature is beneficial for more than just exercise. Outdoor activity has also been found to help reduce stress and improve mental health, heart health, and sleep quality. Some studies even suggest that going for regular hikes can reduce your risk of anxiety, depression, heart disease, and more.

You don't have to do a lot to benefit from getting outdoors. You don't have to go far, and you don't even need to break a sweat. And you definitely don't need to wait for the weekend or your day off. If you work near a park, take a walk on your lunch break to get refreshed. Go for short hikes after work or in the evening as a way to decompress and get some fresh air. Thirty minutes a day is all you need to improve your mental and physical condition.

The forest on Tryon Creek is one of Portland's oldest nature parks.

Main Trail for 0.3 mile. This wide, flat path ambles among dense patches of salmonberry, thimbleberry, lady fern, wood violets, and Oregon grape. In springtime, there is usually a profusion of big white trilliums; the shiny little yellow flowers that adorn the trail almost year-round are buttercups. At the junction with the Red Fox Trail, stay right (west) to continue on the Old Main Trail and descend to Obie's Bridge above Tryon Creek at a little over a half mile.

Once you've crossed the creek, veer left (west) on the West Horse Loop, which climbs easily through more woods. Pass the Cedar Trail and continue to the next junction, veering right (north) to continue on the loop, which now meanders northeast. Continue past the Boones Ferry Horse Trail to the next junction, at 1.2 miles, and turn left (north) toward High Bridge. The path parallels Tryon Creek for a short distance, then crosses the creek on High Bridge. Just across the bridge, veer left (northwest) onto the Lewis and Clark Trail. Back on a narrower path, the way wanders forward on the opposite side of the creek and crosses Terry Riley Bridge at 1.5 miles.

Just across this bridge, turn right (north) and begin a moderate ascent. The path briefly comes alongside a tributary creek, passes a short spur connector to the North Horse Loop, then reaches the top of the Lewis and Clark Trail at 2 miles. Turn right (south) for just a short distance, then veer left (southeast) onto the North Horse Loop. Now back on a wide, level trail, follow the path south, paralleling the paved bike path. At the next junction, at 2.4 miles, turn left (east), then at the very next junction, right (south), to continue toward the nature center. Finally, veer right (south) on the Old Main Trail to complete your hike with a last short ramble through the trees and back to your starting point.

RIDE IT

The trails at Tryon Creek are limited to foot and equestrian use only, however the paved Terwilliger Trail parallels the east side of the park for 3.5 miles, from SW Boones Ferry Road to N. State Street. The path proceeds along the edge of the woods, affording views into the park's interior and tempting you to lock up your bike at the nature center or one of the trailheads and dip inside for a walk under the trees. For a quick sampling of the park, walk the paved, 0.4-mile interpretive Trillium Trail.

Next page: *North Portland's wetlands offer amazing year-round birding (Hike 6).*

NORTH PORTLAND

The North Portland region is not known for its abundance of natural areas. There are a few small community parks, but the region is largely occupied by residential neighborhoods, the sprawling industrial and transportation facilities of the Port of Portland, and, in the case of Sauvie Island, farmland—not exactly the kind of place you might go looking for a path to wander. However, tucked away in this area are a few natural gems in the form of wetlands and wildlife preserves on or near the Columbia and Willamette Rivers.

Each of these natural spaces offers nice walking paths and wooded trails that feature excellent seasonal bird-watching. You can take a riverside stroll to Oregon's smallest lighthouse or see the confluence of the Willamette and Columbia Rivers. Each of these destinations is a mere thirty-minute drive from the central metro area, making any one of them an ideal morning or afternoon outing. And if you're visiting the Sauvie Island locations in summer, give yourself extra time to visit some of the farms to stock up on fresh berries, veggies, and flowers. Though we don't cover it in this guide, paddlers can also check out the Columbia Slough area and its many water trails.

5 Warrior Rock Lighthouse

DISTANCE:	6 miles roundtrip
ELEVATION GAIN:	20 feet
HIGH POINT:	30 feet
DIFFICULTY:	Easy
FITNESS:	Walkers, runners
FAMILY-FRIENDLY:	Suitable for all ages; open shoreline
DOG-FRIENDLY:	Leashed
BIKE-FRIENDLY:	Not permitted
AMENITIES:	Parking, outhouse, beaches
MANAGEMENT:	Oregon Department of Fish and Wildlife (ODFW)
GPS:	N 45° 48.528', W 122° 47.898'
OTHER:	Visitors to Sauvie Island are required to obtain an ODFW day-use permit. Purchase permits at the Cracker Barrel Grocery on the island.

GETTING THERE

Transit: TriMet bus 16 has a station at the Sauvie Island Bridge. From there, it's a 14.4-mile walk or bike ride to the trailhead, so plan accordingly.

Driving: From the downtown area, drive west on US Highway 30 for approximately 9 miles. Turn right on NW Sauvie Island Road, cross the bridge onto the island, and stop at the Cracker Barrel Grocery to pick up your island day pass. From the market, turn right on NW Gillihan Road and drive 5.9 miles through farm country to a fork with NW Reeder Road. Turn right and continue 8.5 miles to the trailhead at the end of the road.

Just a thirty-minute drive from downtown Portland, at the northernmost tip of Sauvie Island, the Multnomah Channel of the Willamette River pours into the mighty Columbia River. Mounted on this sandy point is a small lighthouse. Constructed in 1889, the lighthouse employed an oil lamp and fog beacon in a small wooden structure atop the existing

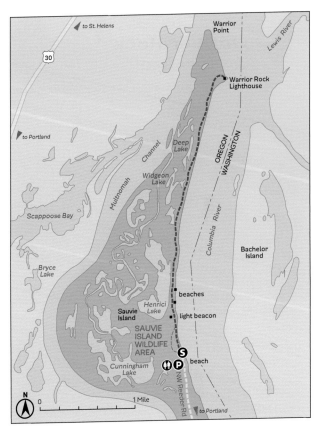

sandstone block base. That wooden structure was replaced by the current octagonal concrete structure in 1930, and the light beacon was converted to electric power. The Warrior Rock Lighthouse is Oregon's smallest lighthouse and one of only two lighthouses still operating in the state that are not on the Pacific coast.

GET MOVING

For a look at the lighthouse and plenty of Columbia River views, start this forested stroll from the end of NW Reeder

Oregon's smallest lighthouse on the Columbia River

Road. The mostly flat trail begins at the parking turnaround through a gated entry. At the trailhead, a short path proceeds right (north) off the main path to a wide, sandy beach. Expect this beach to be crowded on sunny summer weekends, making it worth packing your lunch and beach blanket and opting for one of the other beaches farther along the trail. Since most of the trail is also in moist woodland, it's also advisable to pack along some mosquito repellent in the early summer months.

The trail begins as a gravel road beside a fenced pasture where cows lazily graze in the sun. Where the path enters woodland at 0.2 mile and transitions to an old jeep road, the rest of the route is mostly cool and shaded. Shortly past 0.3 mile, the route forks at a tree-shrouded light beacon tower. Take the right fork to stay on the path to the point. The walking is mostly effortless as the trail wanders under the trees, with a lot of tall grass and snowberry lining the trailside. At 0.5 and 0.6 mile, short side trails branch off to nice beach areas on the Columbia. Unseen, marshy Henrici Lake is through the trees to the left (west) of the trail, hence the need for bug spray.

The easy path continues for the next 2.4 miles mostly under tall cottonwood, Oregon ash, and willow trees. A few grassy clearings showcase summer wildflowers; inland are unseen Widgeon and Deep Lakes. There are also occasional views of the Columbia, where you may spy a variety of water-fowl in riverside wetlands, as well as sailboats, barges, and cargo ships making their way up and down the river. Just before arriving at the end of the road, the trail curves to the right (east), through patches of purple aster, and spills onto the sandy beach at Warrior Point. A short path proceeds along the riverside to the lighthouse. Kick back on the beach, enjoy the breeze and the view, and return by the same route when ready.

6   Oak Island Nature Trail

DISTANCE:	2.7 miles roundtrip
ELEVATION GAIN:	50 feet
HIGH POINT:	30 feet
DIFFICULTY:	Easy
FITNESS:	Walkers, runners
FAMILY-FRIENDLY:	Suitable for all ages; open shoreline
DOG-FRIENDLY:	Leashed
BIKE-FRIENDLY:	Not permitted
AMENITIES:	Parking, interpretive signs, outhouse, picnic area
MANAGEMENT:	Oregon Department of Fish and Wildlife (ODFW)
GPS:	N 45° 42.852', W 122° 49.254'
OTHER:	Visitors to Sauvie Island are required to obtain an ODFW day-use permit. Purchase permits at the Cracker Barrel Grocery on the island.

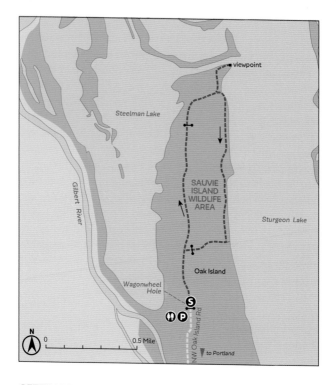

GETTING THERE

Transit: TriMet bus 16 has a station at the Sauvie Island Bridge. From there, it's a 7.4-mile walk or bike ride to the trailhead, so plan accordingly.

   Driving: From the downtown area, drive west on US Highway 30 for approximately 9 miles. Turn right on NW Sauvie Island Road, cross the bridge onto the island, and stop at the Cracker Barrel Grocery to pick up your island day pass. Continue north on NW Sauvie Island Road for 2 miles, then turn right on NW Reeder Road and continue another 1.2 miles. Turn left on NW Oak Island Road and drive 4.2 more miles to the wildlife area at the end of the road.

The Oak Island Nature Trail on Sauvie Island is a place where you can take a walk on the island of an island—although Oak Island is technically a peninsula, with water on three sides. This is a wonderful corner of the 12,000-acre Sauvie Island Wildlife Area, which is a patchwork of grassy fields and oak woodlands and is home to a variety of birds—more than 250 species—and animals. A unique and fun interpretive system employs QR codes to help you identify the preserve's flora and fauna. Just scan the codes with your smartphone (QR code reader app required), and you will be directed to web pages that offer information about island mammals, waterfowl, and natural and cultural features. Visit www.mirrorofnature.bigwhisper.com for more info.

GET MOVING

Start at the gate at the end of NW Oak Island Road. Proceed around the gate and walk straight ahead (north) on an old road under the cover of tall white oaks, with snowberry and Oregon ash lining the path. Look for the first interpretive marker. Where the trail emerges from the trees at 0.3 mile, the loop begins. Continue straight ahead to walk the loop clockwise, with open grassland and Steelman Lake on your left (west) and fenced-in oak woodland on your right (east). Make sure you're peeking into the trees for birds and critters. At 1 mile, the fenced preserve area cuts across the path.

Proceed into the preserve through a side gate and continue straight ahead. If you have your pup along for your walk, it needs to be leashed inside the preserve area. The path starts curving to the right (east), skirting the woods to a wide fork at 1.3 miles. Here, you can take a 0.2-mile side trip to the island's northeastern point for a decent view over the wetlands surrounding Sturgeon Lake. Continuing clockwise on the main path, turn south through a shrubby, viewless corridor. Look for birds both overhead and in the surrounding trees and brush, and more interpretive markers.

Oak Island on Sauvie Island

Where the loop makes its final right (west) turn, at 2.1 miles, a short side trail branches off to the left (east) to the rocky, muddy shore of Sturgeon Lake. There are nice shade trees above the shore to sit and watch for ducks, herons, and raptors. The final stretch proceeds through another grove of shady white oaks, past the last interpretive marker, then through another gate into the open, grassy area where you started the loop. Reconnect with the old gravel road, turn left (south), and retrace your steps back to your starting point.

GO FARTHER

Pack a picnic and enjoy it lakeside. Near the gated trailhead, walk a well-trod short path left (west) across an open pasture

SAUVIE ISLAND WILDLIFE GUIDE

Sauvie Island is home to more than 250 species of nesting and migratory birds. This includes a variety of waterfowl, songbirds, and raptors. Here is a checklist of some of the species you may spot.

- Blackbird
- Chickadee
- Coot
- Cormorant
- Crane
- Dove
- Duck
- Eagle
- Egret
- Finch
- Flicker
- Goose
- Grebe
- Grosbeak
- Gull
- Harrier
- Hawk
- Heron
- Hummingbird
- Jay
- Kestrel
- Kingfisher
- Meadowlark
- Nuthatch
- Oriole
- Owl
- Pelican
- Pigeon
- Pintail
- Plover
- Quail
- Raven
- Robin
- Sandpiper
- Sapsucker
- Scaup
- Snipe
- Sparrow
- Starling
- Swallow
- Teal
- Tern
- Thrush
- Towhee
- Warbler
- Wigeon
- Woodpecker
- Wren

area to the edge of Wagonwheel Hole on Steelman Lake, one of the bodies of water surrounding the "island." Spread your blanket on the rocky beach under shade trees for a pleasant lunch spot.

7 Kelley Point Park

DISTANCE:	2.2 miles of trails
ELEVATION GAIN:	70 feet
HIGH POINT:	50 feet
DIFFICULTY:	Easy
FITNESS:	Walkers, runners, cyclists, barrier-free
FAMILY-FRIENDLY:	Suitable for all ages; open shoreline
DOG-FRIENDLY:	Permitted
BIKE-FRIENDLY:	Permitted
AMENITIES:	Parking, picnic areas, restrooms, interpretive signs, beach, viewpoints
MANAGEMENT:	Portland Parks and Recreation
GPS:	N 45° 38.604', W 122° 45.960'
OTHER:	Park hours 6:00 AM to 10:00 PM; posted signs warn visitors to stay out of the rivers

GETTING THERE

Transit: Take the MAX Yellow Line to the Expo Center station. Walk five minutes north on the pedestrian path to N. Marine Drive. Cross the street at the intersection and pick up TriMet bus 11 westbound. The bus makes a stop 0.3 mile east of the park entrance road. Walk 0.7 mile to the park area.

Driving: From the downtown area, drive north on I-5 for approximately 5 miles. Take exit 307 for westbound Marine Drive; turn right and continue 4.4 miles. Turn right into the park and proceed to the south parking area and trailhead.

Bike: From the Expo Center area, ride 5.5 miles west on the 40-Mile Loop to the park.

At the northwesternmost tip of the Portland metro area, the 187-mile Willamette River completes its journey across western Oregon at its confluence with the mighty Columbia River. Explorers Lewis and Clark missed the Willamette during their first survey of the Columbia's tributaries and had to return

Lewis and Clark missed this point. You shouldn't.

after receiving new directions from the local Natives. Today, all you have to do is input "Kelley Point Park" in your smart-phone, and it will lead you right to the point where these two notable waterways merge and where a pleasant park offers

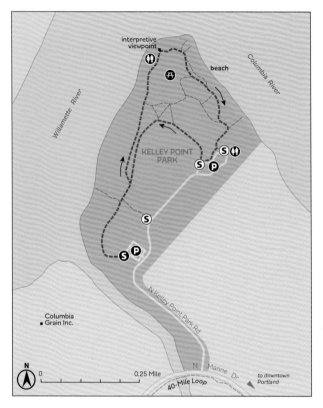

walking trails, picnic grounds, river views, and a wide sandy beach.

GET MOVING

For an easy 1.6-mile lollipop loop that nets you nice views of both rivers, as well as the grassy picnic meadow, start at the south (first) parking area, where you will find the trailhead in the southwest corner. Head down the flat, paved path into a stand of tall cottonwoods. To the south, you'll likely hear the large Columbia Grain mill churning away, visible through the trees; perhaps a huge transport ship will be taking on a load to carry to parts far and wide. The path soon turns north, and the sounds of industry start to fade into the background.

As you amble on, you will begin to spy the Willamette River through the trees left (west) of the trail. Several user trails branch off the main path to descend to the sandy riverside—but take heed of the warning signs to stay out of the water. Where the trail forks, veer left and proceed through a small open meadow, another grove of trees, then enter a wide clearing of gently rolling grassy hills. There are several picnic areas with tables at the fringes of the park, while the open central area is perfect for playing with Fido or tossing a Frisbee.

Just beyond the (seasonal) restroom building, reach the viewpoint at the northernmost point of land. Here, see where the Willamette and Columbia Rivers merge in a vast, watery expanse. Look for container ships and barges making their way upriver to various ports, or downriver to the Pacific. The land across the water to the northwest is Sauvie Island; to the northeast is Washington State. An interpretive sign at the point indicates how Kelley Point received its name and details how Lewis and Clark actually missed this location during their exploration.

The loop continues, now paralleling the Columbia River. There are a handful of good views as the trail meanders above the riverbank, then comes to another restroom building at the edge of the north (second) parking area. Alternatively, if the river level is low, you can walk along the sandy beach for a ways, then reconnect to the main trail via a short spur. To close your loop, proceed through the parking area to the trailhead at the west end, then turn right (north) and duck back into the park. Follow the path as it curves west and then south, now on the other side of the picnic meadows. Where the trail reconnects with the route you came in on, retrace your steps back to your starting point.

8 Smith and Bybee Wetlands

DISTANCE:	1.7 miles roundtrip
ELEVATION GAIN:	50 feet
HIGH POINT:	30 feet
DIFFICULTY:	Easy
FITNESS:	Walkers, cyclists, barrier-free
FAMILY-FRIENDLY:	Suitable for all ages
DOG-FRIENDLY:	Not permitted
BIKE-FRIENDLY:	40-Mile Loop trail only
AMENITIES:	Parking, interpretive signs, restrooms
MANAGEMENT:	Oregon Metro
GPS:	N 45° 36.996', W 122° 43.092'
OTHER:	Park hours sunrise to sunset

Watch for giant dragonflies near rivers and wetlands.

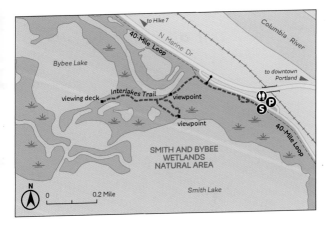

GETTING THERE

Transit: Take the MAX Yellow Line to the Expo Center station. Walk five minutes north on the pedestrian path to N. Marine Drive. Cross the street at the intersection and pick up TriMet bus 11 westbound. The bus makes stops within a few walking minutes of the park entrance.

Driving: From the downtown area, drive north on I-5 for approximately 5 miles. Take exit 307 for westbound Marine Drive; turn right and continue 2.2 miles. Turn left into the park and proceed to the parking area and trailhead.

Bike: From the Expo Center area, ride 2.7 miles west on the 40-Mile Loop to the park.

You would never expect to find a 2000-acre natural area smack in the middle of North Portland's sprawling industrial port complex. But hidden behind a wall of trees lies an oasis of reed canary grass, thistle, and spiraea, two large seasonal lakes, several ponds, and a patchwork of deciduous forest and grassy meadows, which are home to a plethora of wildlife. Before you visit, download the park's bird and wildlife checklists, as well as the seasonal nature guide, then grab your

A birder's paradise, Smith and Bybee Wetlands can be visited year-round.

cameras and binoculars and come explore this hidden gem that offers year-round in-city safari adventures.

GET MOVING

From the parking area, cross the park road to the paved 40-Mile Loop trail and turn right (northwest). Stroll along, with the park road on your right and stands of cottonwoods, willows, and ash on your left. Through the trees, you can catch brief glimpses of Smith Lake, the larger of the wetlands' two lakes. The traffic noise from nearby Marine Drive is distracting, but that will fade into the background soon enough. At 0.3 mile, the path forks, with the 40-Mile Loop branching right and the Interlakes Trail veering left.

Turn onto the Interlakes Trail, where, just a few paces in, a large interpretive sign greets you with information about the area. In addition to a map, the sign offers a list of some of the bird and animal species known to inhabit each of the wetland's unique environments. In the forested areas, look for rabbits, tree frogs, deer, wrens, and owls; in the marshy meadows, look for salamanders, weasels, garter snakes, scrub jays, and goldfinches; and in the lakes and ponds, look for painted turtles, beavers, river otters, herons, and teals—all among many other birds and small mammals. Put your critter goggles on and head in.

The path proceeds into cottonwood forest for 0.2 mile to another fork. To the right is a fenced viewpoint overlooking a small pond; to the left the path heads to the Smith Lake viewpoint. Take a peek at the pond for any wildlife, but save Smith Lake for the return trip. Continue straight ahead (west), past another side trail to Smith Lake, and carry on through the trees and across an open meadow to a viewing deck at the edge of Bybee Lake. Scan the trees and water for ducks, coots, osprey, and eagles. After you've gotten a good look, head back to the second junction you passed and turn right (south).

Take the 0.2-mile side loop through more forest to the edge of Smith Lake. The trail proceeds over a grated walkway to another viewing deck, which, in winter and spring, may be right over the water. The wide view takes in all of the Smith Lake area and beyond to Portland's West Hills. Continue scanning for birds and aquatic wildlife. If you spot a small furry head in the water, it may be a beaver—but it is more likely to be a nutria, a smaller, invasive rodent. Once you've checked off as many species as you can, exit the shelter by way of the opposite side and follow the path back to the main route. From this point, retrace your steps back to the parking area.

Next page: *There are plenty of opportunities to wander under the trees in Portland's Forest Park.*

FOREST PARK

Forest Park is the crown jewel in Portland's urban parks system. Covering an area of more than 5100 acres and stretching for 7 miles in the eastern Tualatin Mountains, it is the largest urban forest in the United States. The concept of a forest preserve in Portland's West Hills reaches all the way back to the 1860s, when Portland's founders recognized the area's potential. When landscape architects John and Frederick Olmsted were hired by the city to beautify Portland for the 1905 Lewis and Clark Expedition centennial, they too recognized how a "forest park" could enhance a burgeoning city in connection with surrounding nature. After more than forty years of development and advocacy, Forest Park was dedicated in 1948.

Blanketing primarily the north side of the range, the forest itself is largely composed of second-growth Douglas fir, western hemlock, western red cedar, big-leaf maple, and vine maple, with a smattering of alder and cottonwood. The lush forest floor is carpeted with, among other things, a variety of ferns, berry shrubs, salal, waterleaf, vanilla leaf, and duckfoot. In spring and summer, wildflowers such as trillium, buttercup, willow herb, self-heal, hawksbeard, yarrow, and herb Robert add splashes of cheerful color to the sun-dappled forest floor. All this—just minutes from the city center—presents countless opportunities for walkers, hikers, trail runners, and mountain bikers to explore Portland's urban wilderness on trails long and short.

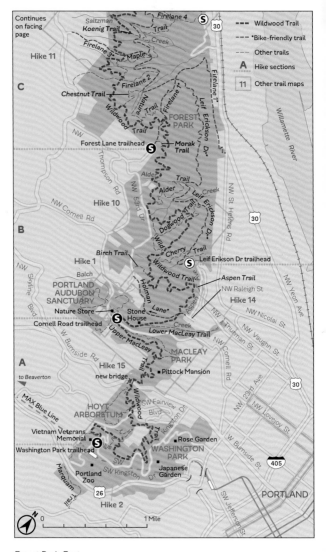

Forest Park, East

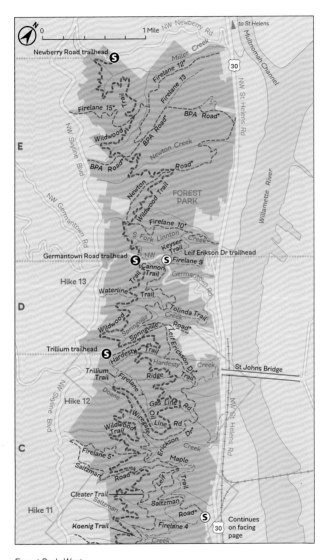

Forest Park, West

9 Wildwood Trail and Leif Erikson Drive

DISTANCE:	41 miles of trails
ELEVATION GAIN:	Up to 3200 feet
HIGH POINT:	970 feet
DIFFICULTY:	Easy to challenging
FITNESS:	Walkers, hikers, runners, equestrians, cyclists
FAMILY-FRIENDLY:	Shorter segments suitable for older children; some steep trails; winter, spring often muddy
DOG-FRIENDLY:	Leashed
BIKE-FRIENDLY:	See Ride the Park
AMENITIES:	Various facilities at Washington Park trailhead, limited parking at most trailheads
MANAGEMENT:	Portland Parks and Recreation
GPS:	N 45° 30.762', W 122° 43.014' (Washington Park)
OTHER:	Park hours 5:00 AM to 10:00 PM. Check the Forest Park Conservancy website for their trail map and visitor's guide

GETTING THERE

Transit: The MAX Red and Blue Lines both stop at Washington Park. From the station, walk a short distance north to the Marquam/Wildwood trailhead, just north of the Vietnam Veterans Memorial. TriMet bus 63 also makes a stop at the Washington Park MAX station.

Driving: Washington Park trailhead: Drive US Highway 26 to exit 72 for the Zoo and Forestry Center; turn north and head up into Washington Park. Veer left on SW Knights Boulevard for the Forestry Center. Proceed past the Forestry Center and Vietnam Veterans Memorial and find parking on the right (east) side of the road at the corner of SW Kingston Drive. Find the Marquam/Wildwood trailhead on the west side of the road. **Cornell Road trailhead:** From Portland's Pearl District, drive west on NW Lovejoy Street approximately 1 mile. Veer right (northwest) at the fork onto NW Cornell

Road. Proceed about 1.5 miles to the trailhead just before the Portland Audubon Sanctuary Nature Store; parking is available on both sides of street. **Forest Lane trailhead:** From the downtown area, drive west on NW Lovejoy Street. At the fork, veer right (northwest) on NW Cornell Road and continue 1.9 miles. Turn right on NW 53rd Drive and go 1.7 miles to gravel Forest Lane; turn right and proceed to the trailhead. **Trillium trailhead:** From the downtown area, drive west on W. Burnside Street through Washington Park for approximately 2.5 miles. Where Burnside forks, veer right (northwest) on NW Skyline Boulevard. Continue on Skyline for 5.5 miles, then turn right (north) on gravel NW Springville Road to the trailhead. **Germantown Road trailhead:** From the downtown area, drive west on US Highway 30 for 5.5 miles. Turn left (west) onto NW Germantown Road and drive 1.6 miles to where the Wildwood Trail crosses the road. **Newberry Road trailhead:**

Leif Erikson Drive through Forest Park

BRIDGE OVER BURNSIDE

Construction will begin on a new pedestrian bridge over W. Burnside Road in 2018. This will eliminate the challenging road crossing in this location and provide a safe and uninterrupted continuation of the Wildwood Trail. Designed by award-winning architect Ed Carpenter, the new bridge will reflect the natural aesthetics of Forest Park. It will be constructed by the Portland Parks Foundation, with funding provided by the city, local businesses and foundations, and community support.

From the Germantown Road trailhead, continue 0.5 mile up NW Germantown Road to NW Skyline Boulevard. Turn right (north) on Skyline and drive 2.6 miles to NW Newberry Road. Turn right (east) and continue 0.7 mile to the trailhead on the right (east) side of the road. (NOTE: NW Newberry Road was closed to traffic in 2017 due to a landslide.)

See Hikes 10–13 for additional access points to the Wildwood via spur trails.

Bike: Ride your way to the Portland Rose Garden in Washington Park on SW Kingston Dr. Continue 1.5 miles south and west to the Marquam/Wildwood trailhead near the Vietnam Veterans Memorial. Or ride 1.3 miles west and south on SW Fairview Boulevard, then turn left (south) on SW Knights Boulevard for 0.3 mile to the trailhead. Bikes not permitted on Wildwood Trail. See "Ride the Park" for directions to the Leif Erikson Drive Trail.

Forest Park's Wildwood Trail is a 30-mile-long walking and hiking route that winds, climbs, descends, and contours the entire east–west length of the park. There are five direct access points to the Wildwood: two on the east side near downtown, two in the middle of the park, and one on the far west side (see Getting There). There are numerous other access points via more than thirty connecting trails, spurs, and fire lanes. This gives you practically unlimited options for creating long and short outings as you like. Hikes 10–13 in this guide will give you some suggestions for several of the trails you can connect with the Wildwood for loops of easy to moderate length and difficulty.

If you have your sights set on hiking the entire Wildwood Trail, the best way is to break it into manageable segments. And since you don't want to have to double back on each segment—unless you want the extra mileage and workout—you'll have to arrange transportation or pickup at each ending point. Public transit might help you out in a few locations, but otherwise you'll need to figure that out on your own. However, once you've completed the entire trail, it will be an impressive notch on your hiking stick.

GET MOVING

Try section-hiking the Wildwood Trail in these manageable pieces.

Section A—Washington Park to Balch Creek: 4.7 miles, +810 feet/-1040 feet

Start at the Washington Park trailhead at the east end of the Wildwood by meandering on fairly gentle grades through the maze of trails in the Hoyt Arboretum (Hike 2); check out a few of the park's flora features, like the sequoia and coast redwood grove. Next, carefully cross W. Burnside Road (see bridge sidebar) and make a moderate ascent to the top of Pittock Hill and its namesake historic mansion (Hike 15); stop to enjoy the views. From there, make a steady descent through shady woods to the trailhead at NW Cornell Road, near the Portland Audubon Sanctuary (Hike 1); stop into the Nature Store for info and nature guides for exploring deeper into Forest Park.

Section B—Balch Creek to Firelane 1: 5.8 miles, +1000/-530 feet

Start at the trailhead on NW Cornell Road and descend to Balch Creek; follow the creek downstream to the Stone House, also known as the Witch's Castle, and take the obligatory photo with the mossy relic (Hike 14). Veer upward to make a moderate, winding ascent before the trail levels for a pleasant walk under shady mixed forest; the way passes the Wild Cherry, Dogwood, and Alder Trails (Hike 10), and contours through several drainages that converge into Alder Creek. Finish with a gentle ascent high on the hillside; veer onto the Morak Trail spur to Firelane 1 and walk the old road to the Forest Lane trailhead.

Section C–Firelane 1 to NW Springville Road: 8.3 miles, +1240/-1150 feet

This longer section will give you a bit more of a workout as you proceed through numerous ups, downs, and creek drainages in the park's central section. Beginning at the Forest Lane trailhead, descend Firelane 1 and the Morak Trail to the Wildwood and proceed through the Maple Trail area (Hike 11); the winding path crosses Rocking Chair, Saltzman, and Doane Creeks. Veer off the Wildwood after crossing the small bridge over Doane Creek and make a hearty ascent on the narrow Trillium Trail to Firelane 7 (Hike 12); turn left (west) and proceed to the Trillium trailhead at the gate on NW Springville Road.

Section D–NW Springville Road to NW Germantown Road: 6.4 miles, +660/-970 feet

Pick up where you left off at the Trillium trailhead on NW Springville Road; head out on Firelane 7 to the Trillium Trail and descend back to the Wildwood. The path then proceeds along a fairly level grade under shady woods through most of the segment. Wind through several more drainage canyons and pass the Ridge and Hardesty Trails, as well as Hardesty Creek; the path also passes a lower portion of the Springville Road Trail. Hook through two more small canyons that feed Springville Creek, then begin a gentle descent that crosses

Forest Park's Wildwood Trail is 30 miles of urban forest bliss.

the Waterline Trail (Hike 13) and ends at the large trailhead at NW Germantown Road.

Section E–NW Germantown Road to NW Newberry Road: 5.1 miles, +700/-830 feet

This final segment of the Wildwood is also the most remote; you may actually find more company with the mountain bikers who crisscross the trail on a handful of bike-friendly routes. Continue west from the NW Germantown Road trailhead where the path rises and falls over moderate terrain to cross South Fork Linnton and Newton Creeks; following the latter, make a big ascent to the BPA Road. Finish with an even bigger descent to cross both forks of Miller Creek, then give yourself a big high-five when you reach the end at the NW Newberry Road trailhead.

RIDE THE PARK

The main route for trail riding in Forest Park is **Leif Erikson Drive**. This 11-mile good, gravel road twists and turns through the park from NW Thurman Street to NW Germantown Road. The road is relatively level, with just gentle ups and downs, which makes it accessible for most riding ages and abilities. From either end, you can ride out and back, or use other bike-friendly trails (see map) that connect to the road to create a variety of loop options. If you choose the latter, get ready for some grinding ascents, sure to work the quads, but getting to rip down the opposite end makes it all worthwhile

For the eastern trailhead, nearest downtown, proceed through the Northwest District to NW Thurman Street. The best access is via NW 23rd Avenue. Turn west and proceed 1.4 miles to the trailhead at the end of the road. For the western trailhead, follow directions to the trailhead on NW Germantown Road.

Holman-Firelane 1 Loop: This 6.7-mile-loop ride starts at the trailhead at the end of NW Raleigh Street. The first 0.8 mile grinds west four hundred feet up Holman Lane (uphill only) to NW 53rd Drive. Turn right (north) and ride the road for 1.3 miles. Just before 53rd ends at NW Thompson Road, turn right (north) on Firelane 1. The path proceeds along the undulating ridgeline for about a half mile—then the fun begins. The first part of the descent follows the ridgeline before switching back to drop into a drainage. At the bottom of the hill, at 3.2 miles, turn right (east) onto Leif Erikson Drive and cruise along. The road turns south and easily contours the hillside under shady forest, turning in and out of small drainages along the way. Around 4.5 miles, the path makes a big, winding turn into a larger canyon, then turns out to contour Dogwood ridge (Hike 10) and ends at 6 miles at the trailhead at NW Thurman Street. To get back to your starting point, ride Thurman 0.1 mile east, then veer onto NW Aspen Avenue for 0.5 mile to its end; turn right (west) on Raleigh to close your loop.

10 Dogwood Loops

DISTANCE:	3.3 miles of trails
ELEVATION GAIN:	310 to 610 feet
HIGH POINT:	900 feet
DIFFICULTY:	Moderate
FITNESS:	Hikers, runners
FAMILY-FRIENDLY:	Suitable for older children
DOG-FRIENDLY:	Leashed
BIKE-FRIENDLY:	Not permitted
AMENITIES:	Street parking
MANAGEMENT:	Portland Parks and Recreation
GPS:	N 45° 32.304', W 122° 44.046'
OTHER:	Park hours 5:00 AM to 10:00 PM

GETTING THERE

Transit: Not available.

   Driving: From the downtown area, drive west on NW Lovejoy Street. At the fork, veer right (northwest) on NW Cornell Road and continue 1.9 miles through MacLeay Park. Turn right on NW 53rd Drive and proceed 0.9 mile to the trailhead on the right (north) side of the road. Parking is available in nearby turnouts.

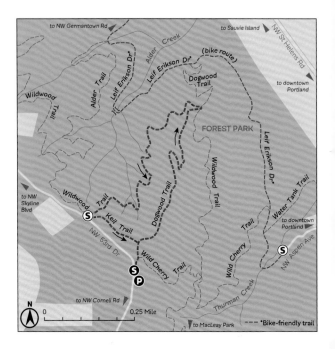

Take in a small sample of Forest Park on a 1.6-mile loop that incorporates the Dogwood, Wildwood, and Keil Trails, with options for creating larger loops if you want to explore more (see Go Farther). Unfortunately, the dogwoods for which this location was christened are gone. Back in the day, this area held a grove of native dogwoods, which were notable for their brilliant white blossoms. Even with their absence, this section of the park still offers plenty of other foliage to admire, including sword and maidenhair fern, Oregon grape, and trillium, all under a shady fir and maple forest.

GET MOVING

From the trailhead on NW 53rd Drive, step onto the Dogwood Trail and head north into Forest Park. After just a few yards, the trail comes to a wide junction where the Wild Cherry Trail branches off to the right (east), and just a few yards farther, the Keil Trail forks off to the left (west). The former is one of the options for creating a larger loop (see Go Farther); the latter is the return route at the end of this loop. Proceed straight through both of these junctions and begin a short ascent to one of Forest Park's highest points. Here, at the crest that was once known as Inspiration Point, there used to be a view of downtown Portland. That view is now obstructed by trees.

Now begin a steady descent north along the ridgeline, deviating only to pass through a couple of switchbacks. The descent comes to an end shortly past the 0.6-mile mark at a wide junction with the Wildwood Trail. The Dogwood Trail continues descending another 0.4 mile to Leif Erikson Drive (see Go Farther), but instead, turn left (west) onto the Wildwood Trail and begin an easier ascent along the flank of the ridge you just descended. The trail contours generally south along the ridge, dipping inward numerous times to skirt small springs and drainages. Approaching 1.4 miles, the Wildwood

The dogwoods are gone, but there is plenty more to enjoy on this trail.

meets the Keil Trail at a junction right near the road. Veer left (east) onto this spur trail and make a short ascent back to the junction where you started.

GO FARTHER

You have two options for creating larger loops from this trailhead. The first is a 2.9-mile loop that incorporates the Dogwood and Alder Trails. Descend the Dogwood Trail for 1 mile, passing the Wildwood Trail, to Leif Erikson Drive. Turn left (west) and walk along Leif Erikson for 0.5 mile to the Alder Trail. Turn left (west) onto the Alder Trail and climb gradually for 0.8 mile to meet the Wildwood again at 2.4 miles. Turn left (east) and proceed a level 0.3 mile to the Keil Trail junction; veer right on the Keil Trail for the final 0.3 mile back to your starting point.

You can go even farther by creating a grand 3.3-mile loop incorporating the Wild Cherry, Leif Erikson, Alder, and Wildwood Trails. Starting at the same Dogwood trailhead, veer right (east) onto the Wild Cherry Trail for a steady 0.8-mile descent, passing the Wildwood Trail, to Leif Erikson Drive. Turn left (north) and make a gentle ascent on Leif Erikson for 1.2 miles. Along the way, it dips deep into the drainage for Alder Creek. Near the 2-mile mark, turn left (west) onto the Alder Trail and follow the same directions as above for the final stretch.

11   Maple Loops

DISTANCE:	8.5 miles of trails
ELEVATION GAIN:	940 to 1130 feet
HIGH POINT:	890 feet
DIFFICULTY:	Moderate
FITNESS:	Hikers, runners
FAMILY-FRIENDLY:	Suitable for older children
DOG-FRIENDLY:	Leashed

BIKE-FRIENDLY:	Not permitted
AMENITIES:	Trailhead parking
MANAGEMENT:	Portland Parks and Recreation
GPS:	N 45° 33.984', W 122° 45.204'
OTHER:	Park hours 5:00 AM to 10:00 PM

GETTING THERE

Transit: TriMet bus 16 stops near the corner of NW St. Helens and NW Saltzman Roads. Walk 0.7 mile up NW Saltzman to the trailhead.

Driving: From the downtown area, drive west on US Highway 30 toward St. Helens for approximately 3.5 miles. Turn left (west) onto NW Saltzman Road and proceed 0.7 mile to the gated trailhead at the end of the road.

This large circuit on the east slope of Forest Park utilizes the Maple and Wildwood Trails for an 8.5-mile exploration of a couple of the park's larger, central drainages—Saltzman and Maple Creeks—as well as some of the nicest woodland in the entire park. The full route twists and turns through several unique sections of the park, offering a variety of bird- and leaf-peeping. Don't have time for the full loop? Cut the mileage down by using one of the many cutoff trails along the way for shorter loop options (see Go Shorter).

GET MOVING

Begin by walking around the road gate and proceed up gravel Saltzman Road for 0.5 mile. The roadside is lined with thimbleberry, sword fern, vanilla leaf, vine maple, and bleeding heart. Where the Maple Trail crosses the road, start your loop by veering left (south) onto the Maple Trail and begin a moderate ascent under shady alder, maple, cedar, and fir trees. The trail eases and meanders through berry shrubs to cross Saltzman Creek at 1.4 miles. At 1.5 miles is the junction with the Koenig Trail. This is one of the options for doing a shorter loop (see Go Shorter).

Continue on the Maple Trail, now ascending steadily, and cross several small springs and tributaries. At 1.9 miles, cross wide gravel Leif Erikson Drive and continue ascending. The way is mostly cool and shady under the dense, mossy canopy; groundcover now shows maidenhair fern, salal, and Oregon grape. At 2.3 miles, bypass a cutoff spur and dip down to cross Munger Creek. At 2.7 miles, the Maple Trail ends at a junction with the Wildwood Trail. Turn right (north) onto the Wildwood, which now becomes your main path for

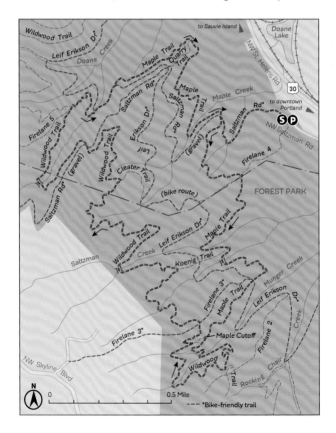

Choose your own adventure on Forest Park's Maple Trail.

the next 3.7 miles. The route now takes a gentler, zigzagging way northwest, contouring ridges and dipping into narrow creek canyons.

As you cruise comfortably along, keep your eyes peeled for a variety of birds in the trees, including woodpeckers. In the spring, look for bright white trillium and orange Columbia lily. At 5.2 miles is your second option for a shorter loop: the Cleater Trail (see Go Shorter). Continuing on the Wildwood, contour another ridge, dive deep into a tributary canyon for Doane Creek, then come to a forklike junction with Firelane 5 at 6.4 miles. Now, veer right (east) off the Wildwood and descend the steep fire lane for 0.3 mile to Leif Erikson Drive. Veer right and walk the road for 0.2 mile to a bend in the road where you can pick up the other end of the Maple Trail. Turn left (north) onto the Maple Trail and contour the lower slope, first east, then south, cross Maple Creek and reconnect to Saltzman Road at 8 miles. Turn left (south) and proceed back down the road to the trailhead.

GO SHORTER

If you don't have time for the full loop, or if you have young-sters or a dog in tow, cut off one or both ends of the loop for shorter options. On the south side, use the Koenig Trail between the Maple and the Wildwood. On the north side, from the Wildwood Trail, use the Cleater Trail and Leif Erikson Drive to connect with Saltzman Road or the Quarry and Maple Trails. This cuts the distance down to 5.5 miles. There are sev-eral other options to mix and match connecting trails for even longer or shorter outings.

12   Trillium Loops

DISTANCE:	4.6 miles of trails
ELEVATION GAIN:	Up to 730 feet
HIGH POINT:	1080 feet
DIFFICULTY:	Moderate
FITNESS:	Hikers, runners
FAMILY-FRIENDLY:	Suitable for older children
DOG-FRIENDLY:	Leashed
BIKE-FRIENDLY:	Not permitted
AMENITIES:	Trailhead parking
MANAGEMENT:	Portland Parks and Recreation
GPS:	N 45° 34.470', W 122° 47.334'
OTHER:	Park hours 5:00 AM to 10:00 PM

GETTING THERE

Transit: Not available.

Driving: From the downtown area, drive west on W. Burn-side Street through Washington Park for approximately 2.5 miles. Where Burnside forks, veer right (northwest) on NW Skyline Boulevard. Continue on Skyline for 5.5 miles, then turn right (north) on gravel NW Springville Road to the trailhead.

Forest Park's Trillium Trail is just a short connector spur to access the longer Wildwood Trail (Hike 9). From this access point, however, there are numerous opportunities for exploring this portion of the park on loop trails ranging from 2.3 miles to 4.6 miles. This particular section of the park provides ample opportunity to rehike the area's trails, with options for everything from a quick ridge run to a longer forest stroll. The following description outlines the longest loop option, with info on alternate options along the way.

GET MOVING

Proceed past the road gate and head down gravel NW Springville Road for 50 yards to a wide fork and veer right onto Firelane 7; the left fork, Springville Road, will be your return route. The way forward descends into the park, with plenty of mossy big-leaf maples overhead and blackberry, buttercup, and Pacific waterleaf along the trailside. After just 0.1 mile, the Hardesty Trail drops off the ridgetop to the left (north; see Alternatives); just beyond, at 0.2 mile, the Trillium Trail drops

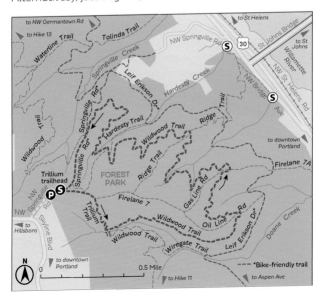

Get deep into Forest Park on the Trillium Trail.

off the ridgetop to the right (south). Turn onto this narrow track and begin a steep, 0.2-mile descent. Watch for itinerant roots looking to catch your toes. The trail bottoms out beside trickling Doane Creek at a junction with the Wildwood Trail.

Here, at 0.4 mile, turn left (east) on the Wildwood and begin your cruise through the park. The trail largely sticks to the slope's contour, keeping mostly level as the drainage falls away to your right (south), becoming noticeably deeper. The trail makes a northward bend and crosses Oil Line Road at 1.3 miles (see Alternatives). Continue forward on the Wildwood, snaking your way through one drainage after another. The trail remains pleasantly flat, allowing you to stroll along and enjoy your surroundings. Ferns, Oregon grape, trillium, wild ginger, waterleaf, duckfoot, candy flower, and self-heal carpet the trailside and slopes; thimbleberry, salmonberry, and vine maple rise above that; and big-leaf maple, Douglas fir, and western red cedar tower overhead.

Continue on the Wildwood for another 3 miles, crossing Fire-lane 7A and the Ridge and Hardesty Trails (see Alternatives), until the trail reaches NW Springville Road at 4.3 miles. Turn left (south) and proceed 0.3 mile up the old roadbed alongside creeping blackberry shrubs. The road bends westward and levels out, depositing you at the top of the ridge and back at the fork where you began your trek. Veer right (west) and proceed back down the road, around the gate, and return to the parking area.

ALTERNATIVES

The number of lateral trails within this loop present several options to shorten the loop if you're looking for a quicker outing, for a change of scenery, or for different workout options. All of these options start the same way, via the Trillium to Wildwood Trail. Cut it down to a 2.3-mile lollipop loop by returning via Oil Line Road to Firelane 7. Go for slightly wider loops using Gas Line Road for 2.8 miles, the Ridge Trail for 3.5 miles, or the Hardesty Trail for 3.9 miles. When you've exhausted those options, change the scenery again with a 4-mile loop using Leif Erikson Drive. Start down the Trillium Trail, then turn right (south) on the Wildwood. Take this a short distance to the Wiregate Trail and use that to jog down to Leif Erikson Drive. Turn left (east) and walk the gravel road to Springville Road. Turn left (south) and head up Springville to close the loop.

13 Waterline Loops

DISTANCE:	5.1 miles of trails
ELEVATION GAIN:	Up to 850 feet
HIGH POINT:	880 feet
DIFFICULTY:	Moderate to difficult
FITNESS:	Hikers, runners, cyclists
FAMILY-FRIENDLY:	Suitable for older children; some steep trails
DOG-FRIENDLY:	Leashed

BIKE-FRIENDLY: Leif Erikson Drive and Springville Road only
AMENITIES: Parking, map and info board, outhouse 100 yards
up trail
MANAGEMENT: Portland Parks and Recreation
GPS: N 45° 35.322', W 122° 47.436'
OTHER: Park hours 5:00 AM to 10:00 PM

GETTING THERE

Transit: TriMet bus 16 stops at the bottom of NW Germantown Road. Walk 0.3 mile up the road to the Tolinda trailhead.
Hike 0.8 mile up the Tolinda Trail to Leif Erikson Drive and
begin your loop from there.

Driving: From the downtown area, drive west on US Highway 30 for 5.5 miles. Turn left (west) for the St. Johns Bridge

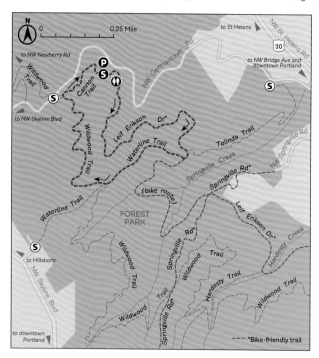

and NW Germantown Road, then make another left onto NW
Bridge Avenue. After turning, make a sharp right turn to proceed up NW Germantown Road and proceed 1.3 miles to the
large trailhead parking area on the left.

Can't decide what to hike in Forest Park? Try a 2.1-mile trail
sampler that gives you a taste of several of the trail types in
the park. The selection includes a casual stroll on old gravel
road, a little cardio on one of the many steep laterals that
cross the park, a bite-size piece of the park's signature zigzagging trail that runs from one end of the park to the other, and
a quick jaunt down a narrow spur connector. Each segment
offers its own unique look at the park and its varied terrain,
whetting your appetite to go longer and farther.

GET MOVING
Near the back (east) of the U-shaped parking area, near a
large map and info board, Leif Erikson Drive proceeds up into
the park. This 11-mile dirt and gravel artery through Forest
Park was once intended to provide access to housing developments on the park's forested slopes. Once it was discovered
how unstable the hillsides could be, the cost to maintain the
road proved to be the development's undoing, and the land
was ceded to the city. Today, it provides a main corridor for
walkers, hikers, runners, and mountain bikers to explore and
enjoy the park on a graded, meandering, gently undulating
track. This is where your hike begins. Start up the road and
enjoy the birds chirping overhead in the big-leaf maples as
you stroll among a variety of ferns, salmonberry, buttercup,
hedge nettle, Pacific waterleaf, and false lily-of-the-valley.

Just as you're getting your groove on, the Tolinda Trail
drops down the ridge to the left (east) at 0.9 mile. Just around
the bend, the Waterline Trail climbs steeply up to the right
(west). Now it's time to pay the piper. Turn onto the Waterline Trail and start a steady, steep ascent of the ridgeline.

Walk under bigleaf maples in Forest Park.

You may notice you're now surrounded by an abundance of Oregon grape and salal. The grade eases for a short stretch, dips down from a slight crest, then resumes its upward trajectory. Halfway up, at 1.3 miles, you suddenly find another trail bisecting your path: the Wildwood Trail. Your workout now finished, veer right (west) onto the Wildwood for your next trail sampling and to continue your loop.

Now on Forest Park's 30-mile end-to-end trail, enjoy a casual stroll higher on the park's eastern slope. The path contours the hillside northward on a gently undulating downgrade, snaking in and out of small drainages. The dense canopy of big-leaf maple, Douglas fir, and red cedar overhead filters the sunlight, keeping the forest shady and cool. Here, maidenhair fern, salmonberry, fringe cup, and Oregon grape thrive. Just as you find your stride and begin indulging in your surroundings, the final junction comes up at 1.8 miles. Here, at an unsigned fork, descend to the right (northwest) on a short spur to a T-junction with the Cannon Trail. Close your loop by turning right (east) on narrow tread that parallels NW Germantown Road as it descends 0.3 mile through swathes of vanilla leaf and thimbleberry and ends near the entrance of the parking area.

GO FARTHER

Want more of a trail buffet than a sampler? Double your mileage into a 4.3-mile loop by passing the Waterline Trail for 1.7 miles and continuing to Springville Road. Get your cardio with a 0.4-mile climb up the gravel road, then veer right onto the Wildwood Trail at 2.1 miles. Now you can enjoy an even longer romp on the Wildwood as it curves through two larger creek ravines before crossing the Waterline Trail at 3.5 miles. Finish the loop by proceeding to the Cannon Trail as above.

Want to mix it up even more and get the Waterline Trail back on the menu? Do a 5.1-mile figure eight by heading up the Leif Erikson and Waterline Trails, then turn left (south) on the Wildwood. Proceed to Springville Road and descend to Leif Erikson, then turn left (west) and walk back to the Waterline. Proceed back up the Waterline a second time (double cardio!), then turn right (west) on the Wildwood and close the figure eight via the Cannon Trail. Sufficiently filled with trail goodness, treat yourself to a milkshake for dessert.

Next page: *Downtown and Mount St. Helens view from Council Crest (Hike 16)*

PORTLAND WEST

On the eastern fringes of Portland's West Hills, and just above the downtown area, the communities of Kings, Arlington, Portland, and Healy Heights are fortunate to enjoy several parks and trail networks right on their doorstep—and some of these sport the best and highest viewpoints over the metro area and beyond. From high atop Council Crest (Hike 16) and Pittock Hill (Hike 15), you can hope to catch one of Portland's acclaimed five-mountain days. That's when the weather is clear enough that you can identify (south to north) Mounts Jefferson, Hood, Adams, St. Helens, and Rainier. But even on less-than-ideal mountain-viewing days, the trail tromping is always exceptional.

The centerpiece among these destinations is Washington Park, home of the Hoyt Arboretum (Hike 2) and the eastern terminus of Forest Park's Wildwood Trail (Hike 9). Connecting with this area is the Marquam Trail to the south and the MacLeay Trails to the north, each of which have their own networks of connecting routes for wandering in pleasantly shady woods boasting dribbling creeks, spring and summer wildflowers, and plenty of bird- and leaf-peeping. Once you've walked a few, see how you can change up your next outings to go longer and farther—the options are practically limitless.

14

Lower MacLeay Park: Balch Creek

DISTANCE:	2.2 miles roundtrip
ELEVATION GAIN:	360 feet
HIGH POINT:	400 feet
DIFFICULTY:	Moderate
FITNESS:	Hikers, runners, some barrier-free
FAMILY-FRIENDLY:	Suitable for all ages
DOG-FRIENDLY:	Leashed
BIKE-FRIENDLY:	Not permitted
AMENITIES:	Trailhead parking, restrooms, picnic area
MANAGEMENT:	Portland Parks and Recreation
GPS:	N 45° 32.130', W 122° 42.750'
OTHER:	Park hours 5:00 AM to 10:00 PM

GETTING THERE

Transit: TriMet bus 15 stops near MacLeay Park at NW 29th and NW 31st Avenues. Take the stairs at the bridge to the park.

Driving: From W. Burnside Street in the Northwest area, drive NW 23rd Avenue north to NW Thurman Street. Turn left (west) and continue 0.5 mile to NW 28th Avenue. Turn right for one block, then left on NW Upshur Street. Proceed 0.2 mile to the park at the parking turnaround.

The hike up Lower MacLeay Trail along Balch Creek is about as straightforward as you can get—that is, it just goes straight. Yet while the trail itself may lack the twists and turns of its neighboring Forest Park trails, the area it passes through is rich in both cultural and natural history. This is most notable in its name, being that of Danford Balch, a local homesteader who was hanged in 1859 for shooting the scoundrel who absconded with his fifteen-year-old daughter. Balch has the notoriety of being the first person to receive capital punishment in Oregon. Throw in one of Oregon's tallest Douglas firs and a witch's castle, and you have a trail worth exploring.

GET MOVING

From the trailhead on NW Upshur Street, head up the wide, paved path, passing under the NW Thurman Street bridge, and up the wooded canyon. The farther you go, the higher and steeper the canyon walls get, adorned with moss-draped Douglas firs, western hemlocks, and western red cedars. Below the trail, Balch Creek trickles and babbles down its rocky gully of partially exposed volcanic basalt. Springtime brings color to the stream banks and hillsides with white trilliums, yellow wood violets, and pale pink toothwort. About a half-mile up the canyon, after the path has crossed the creek, and crossed back, and the pavement has turned to dirt and gravel, look for a particularly large tree to the left (south) of the trail. This is one of Portland's Heritage Trees and is believed to be one of the city's tallest Douglas firs. If undisturbed by fire and storms, this tree could live to be one thousand years old.

About three-quarters of a mile up the canyon, is perhaps Balch Creek's most notable point of interest: the Stone House—or, more hauntingly, the Witch's Castle. In actuality,

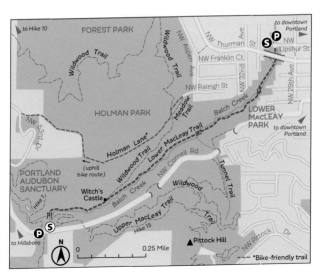

The Witch's Castle on Balch Creek

its history is not as romantic or fearsome as those names imply; it is just an old restroom. It was built in the 1930s by the Works Progress Administration as a rest house for hikers. However, in 1962, a windstorm blew the roof off the building. Since then, it's been gutted and abandoned and left for nature to reclaim. Now it's a favorite mossy relic for kids to climb on and visitors to snap selfies with. Unfortunately, recently, it's also become a popular target for graffiti artists. Near it, the Wildwood Trail branches off to the right. Beyond the Stone House, at 1.1 miles, a bridge crosses the creek and the trail switchbacks up the side of the canyon to NW Cornell Road. If you've gotten your fill, this makes a good turnaround point.

Just do an about-face and follow the creek back down the canyon to your starting point.

GO FARTHER

If you've just gotten your groove on and want to go farther, cross the upper bridge on Balch Creek and switchback up to the trailhead and parking area on NW Cornell Road. Here, you have two options for further roaming: (1) Proceed across the road (south) on the Wildwood Trail and climb Pittock Hill on the Upper MacLeay Trail (Hike 15) to Pittock Mansion and a viewpoint that takes in the whole city—and some of Oregon and Washington's Cascade peaks; or (2) turn right (west) and proceed through the parking area to the Portland Audubon Sanctuary (Hike 1) for more trees, more trails, and a chance to peek into the sanctuary's Wildlife Care Center and see who the current residents are—oftentimes birds of prey or small mammals.

15 Upper MacLeay Park: Pittock Hill

DISTANCE:	2.7 miles of trails
ELEVATION GAIN:	500 feet
HIGH POINT:	956 feet
DIFFICULTY:	Moderate
FITNESS:	Hikers, runners
FAMILY-FRIENDLY:	Suitable for older children
DOG-FRIENDLY:	Leashed
BIKE-FRIENDLY:	Not permitted
AMENITIES:	Parking, picnic area, historical site, viewpoint
MANAGEMENT:	Portland Parks and Recreation
GPS:	N 45° 31.614', W 122° 43.602'
OTHER:	Park hours 5:00 AM to 10:00 PM. Pittock Mansion hours 10:00 AM to 5:00 PM in summer, 10:00 AM to 4:00 PM rest of year; closed holidays and January; admission fee.

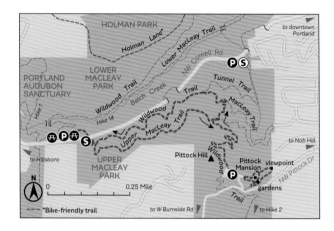

GETTING THERE

Transit: TriMet bus 18 stops at the corner of NW Cornell Road and NW Westover Road. Walk 0.9 mile west on Cornell to MacLeay Park trailheads.

Driving: From the Pearl District, drive west on NW Lovejoy Street approximately 1 mile. Veer right (northwest) at the fork onto NW Cornell Road. Proceed 1.4 miles to MacLeay Park parking area; parking also available on roadside.

Ready for some cardio? The lower portion of MacLeay Park is where you get the nice, casual comfort cruise. Here is where the trail gets down to business. That makes this a great destination when you're looking for a short workout before or after work or if you're in the mood for a good hill climb to a prime viewpoint—without having to go far to get to it. Using one of two trail options, the steady ascent is under mature and pleasantly shady Douglas firs and hemlocks, which is nice for keeping you cool while you climb. There are also enough side and connecting trails so that you can change up your route on repeat visits, or extend your hike if you're in the mood for more mileage.

GET MOVING

Begin at the large parking area on NW Cornell Road. Hop on the Wildwood Trail, which passes right in front of the parking area, and head right (east). In summertime, this short portion of open trail is often decorated with bright white daisies, yellow goldenrod, and pink thistle. The path curves around to cross the road—look both ways! Now it's time to put your game face on. The Wildwood switchbacks up into the forest and quickly comes to a junction with the Upper MacLeay Trail. Both routes lead to the top, however the MacLeay route is a little quieter. Veer right (south) on this path and save the Wildwood for the descent—then, next time, switch it up by doing it in reverse.

The next 0.2 mile is a steady ascent to gain the slopeside. Sun trickles in through the canopy, dappling the area with disco-ball-like shimmers, but otherwise it stays mostly cool and shady. Alongside the trail is the usual mix of flora common to Forest Park: sword, lady, and maidenhair ferns,

Grind up the Upper MacLeay Trail to Pittock Hill.

Oregon grape, fringe cup, duckfoot, foamflower, Pacific water-leaf, vanilla leaf, and trillium. After gaining a couple hundred feet, the grade eases and the trail commences a gentle, contouring ascent of the slope. The trail eventually turns east to head deeper into the forest and comes to a four-way junction near 0.6 mile, where the Wildwood Trail crosses your path. Continue by turning right (east) onto the Wildwood and resume ascending through a series of sweeping switchbacks. After another good uphill sprint, the trail eases again to exit the forest at 1 mile, at the Pittock Mansion parking area.

Turn left (east) and proceed through the parking area to the mansion gate. Here, you can purchase admission to enter the restored French Renaissance–style chateau and witness how Portland's upper crust lived nearly a century ago. You can also walk the grounds (for free) and explore the gardens that showcase a variety of Pacific Northwest plants and flowers, or take in the expansive view from the edge of the bluff. On clear days, you can spot Mounts Hood, Jefferson, St. Helens, Rainier, and Adams. When you're ready to return, proceed back down the Wildwood Trail to the four-way junction. Continue straight through on the Wildwood for a change of scenery on your way down, or for a longer walk make a wider return loop by turning right (east) on the MacLeay Trail (see Go Farther).

GO FARTHER

It's not much, but if you want to add a little extra mileage to your hike, add a 0.6-mile side loop in the middle of heading up or down—or both, for an additional 1.2 miles. You can access the loop from both the Wildwood on the low side and the Upper MacLeay–Wildwood junction on the high side; just fork left (east) from either junction heading up, or right heading down. Either way, the Macleay Trail easily contours the slope side under more pleasant, mature forest, and it makes a wide circuit of a wooded glen where seasonal creeks trickle down the hillside. The trail makes a U-turn at the park boundary, sending you back to the main junctions.

Marquam Nature Park: North Loop and Council Crest

16

DISTANCE:	3.8 miles of trails
ELEVATION GAIN:	Up to 860 feet
HIGH POINT:	Up to 1060 feet
DIFFICULTY:	Moderate
FITNESS:	Hikers, runners
FAMILY-FRIENDLY:	Suitable for older children; some steep trails
DOG-FRIENDLY:	Leashed
BIKE-FRIENDLY:	Not permitted
AMENITIES:	Parking, picnic shelter, interpretive info
MANAGEMENT:	Portland Parks and Recreation
GPS:	N 45° 30.162', W 122° 41.454'
OTHER:	Park hours 5:00 AM to midnight; trailhead parking limited to two hours

GETTING THERE

Transit: TriMet buses 8 and 68 stop at SW Sam Jackson Park Road and Terwilliger Boulevard. Walk 0.2 mile west on SW Sam Jackson Park Road to the park entrance and trailhead.

Driving: From downtown Portland, drive 0.3 mile south on Terwilliger Boulevard. At the signal, continue straight on SW Sam Jackson Park Road for 0.2 mile, then veer right into the park parking area.

Bike: Ride the Terwilliger Trail south from the downtown area, or north from southwest area neighborhoods, to SW Sam Jackson Park Road. Turn right for 0.2 mile, then right again to the trailhead.

Marquam Nature Park is a 200-acre forested hillside above the west bank of the Willamette River and is Portland's third-largest park. Dedicated in 1983, the park was created by donations of private land as a way to keep the lush hillside from becoming overly developed, and as a preserve for native

Start your hike near the Marquam Mosaic.

plants and animals. More than 7 miles of trails weave their way around the hillside in two main sections (also see Hike 17) under mossy big-leaf maples and amid ample ferns, Oregon grape, and thimbleberry. You will also find an abundance of invasive blackberry and English ivy.

Before your hike, take a moment to admire the Marquam Mosaic at the trailhead shelter. It was created by more than four hundred volunteers, under the lead of Portland artist Lynn Takata. The colorful stepped artwork celebrates the diversity of flora and fauna found within the park. You can also pick up a park map from one of the brochure boxes at the shelter. This will come in handy to guide you through the many trail junctions you will encounter along the way. Instead of discarding

IN A PLACE WHERE LISTENING AND LOOKING INSPIRE US

your trail guide when you're finished, please return it to the box for future visitor use.

GET MOVING

Begin your hike by heading uphill to the right (northwest) on the 4T Trail (also called the Shelter Loop Trail) toward Council Crest. The trail surface begins as old roadbed, noticeable by the broken-up chunks of asphalt; it eventually transitions to soft, duffy trail tread. Just after beginning, an easy-to-miss junction with the Sunnyside Trail branches off to the right (north). This trail could be utilized if you desire a slightly longer loop option. Following the junction, the 4T Trail climbs a dense and shrubby drainage on a moderate grade. The little

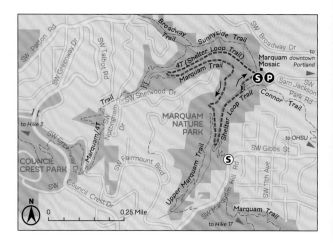

pink flowers at your feet—cute as they may be—are herb Robert, a noxious and invasive geranium.

After a couple of switchbacks to gain the slopeside, the trail comes to a T-junction with the Marquam Trail at 0.4 mile. For a huffing, puffing climb to Council Crest, turn right (see Go Farther); to continue the loop, turn left (east). The trail now contours around the hillside, gently undulating on a comfortable downward slope. Turning south, the route heads into the next drainage and crosses a tiny trickling spring. At 0.9 mile, the Upper Marquam Trail branches upward to the right (north); continue straight, downhill (south). The path continues another 0.1 mile, descends a few steps, then arrives at a wide junction on an old, rocky roadbed.

Turn left (north) and proceed downhill for the last 0.3 mile on the old road, alongside a rocky drainage channel. You may find the air noticeably cooler as you traverse the floor of the shady drainage; look for cute little yellow buttercups adorning the trailside. Near the bottom, pass the Connor Trail, which climbs upward to the right (east) and proceeds 0.5 mile to the Oregon Health and Science University campus. The final stretch becomes smooth, easy walking back to your starting point.

GO FARTHER

Of course, you can drive to the top of Council Crest to take in the great views over downtown Portland and distant Mounts Hood, St. Helens, Adams, and Rainier, but why do that when you can earn the view by climbing to it? At 0.4 mile, at the junction with the Marquam Trail, turn right and make a steady 1.2-mile ascent to the top. The trail winds upward through a quiet wooded community, crosses several roads, then makes a circuitous final ascent to Council Crest Park. After enjoying the view, return via the same route to the Marquam–Shelter Loop junction and finish by completing the loop as described above, or just retrace your steps back down the way you came.

17 Marquam Nature Park: South Loop

DISTANCE:	1.7 miles roundtrip
ELEVATION GAIN:	430 feet
HIGH POINT:	650 feet
DIFFICULTY:	Moderate
FITNESS:	Walkers, hikers, runners
FAMILY-FRIENDLY:	Suitable for all ages; many bridges
DOG-FRIENDLY:	Leashed
BIKE-FRIENDLY:	Not permitted
AMENITIES:	Street parking
MANAGEMENT:	Portland Parks and Recreation
GPS:	N 45º 29.466', W 122º 41.220'
OTHER:	Park hours 5:00 AM to midnight; trailhead parking limited to two hours

GETTING THERE

Transit: TriMet bus 65 stops at SW Terwilliger Boulevard and SW Bancroft Terrace. Walk 0.2 mile south on Terwilliger to the trailhead.

Driving: From downtown Portland, drive 1.8 miles south on SW Terwilliger Boulevard. Look for parking turnouts on both sides of the street. Ignore the brushy trailhead right at the west-side parking area; walk the gravelly sidewalk 100 yards north to the signed trailhead.

Bike: Ride the Terwilliger Trail south from the downtown area, or north from southwest area neighborhoods.

The south side of Marquam Nature Park sees less trail traffic than its northern region and is the place to go if you're looking for a quiet stroll in the woods. Here, mossy big-leaf maples and Douglas firs shelter dense patches of thimbleberry, sword fern, and vine maple while small creeks and springs dribble down the lush hillsides. Among all this green, sandwiched between the Willamette River and the Southwest Hills, and just south of downtown, you can stretch your legs in a natural setting without having to leave the city.

GET MOVING

Begin at the signed Marquam trailhead on the west side of SW Terwilliger Boulevard. The trail begins westward with a

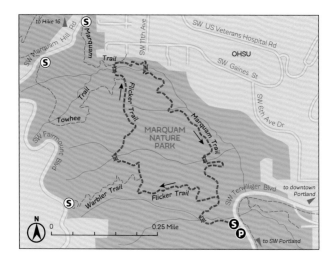

Stroll through quiet woods on the Marquam Trail.

gentle ascent of a lush, shady drainage. An abundance of thimbleberry, with its large, silky leaves, lines the trailside. In spring, thimbleberry blooms with white tissue-paper-like flowers. By summer, those flowers turn into sweet, raspberry-like fruit. The route turns north, crosses a couple of creek beds on sturdy bridges, and comes to a junction at 0.2 mile. This begins the trail loop.

Turn left (west) on the Flicker Trail and proceed deeper into the wooded park. Listen for a variety of birdsong and the tap-tap-tap of woodpeckers. The broad canopy of bigleaf maple, Douglas fir, red cedar, and western hemlock keeps the trail mostly cool and shady. The English ivy that you see among the slopes and climbing the trees is an invasive species. Despite its pleasing green appearance, it actually chokes

Spring brings plenty of trilliums to Portland's parks.

out many native plants. Volunteer crews work diligently every summer to keep it from spreading.

At 0.5 mile, the Warbler Trail branches off to the left (west); continue north on the Flicker Trail. The route continues to wind along through the ferns and Oregon grape, crosses another creek bed on another bridge, and comes to the next junction at 0.8 mile. Here, the Towhee Trail forks off to the left (west) to

SW Marquam Hill Road; continue right (north) to remain on the Flicker Trail. In short order, the trail crosses a large bridge over a gurgling creek, then arrives at a big junction, reconnecting with the Marquam Trail. To the left (west), the trail proceeds into the northern portion of the park (Hike 16) and on to Council Crest. A nearby bench offers the opportunity to sit, look, and listen.

To complete the loop, turn right at the Marquam junction and continue down the drainage. The path proceeds across several more creeks and springs on good bridges, winding its way mostly downhill on easy grade. At one point, the trail forks where the original path has collapsed into the streambed below. Fork right, upslope, around a few trees and reconnect with the main trail 20 yards farther down. After a few more twists and turns, at 1.5 miles, you're back at the junction where you started the loop. Take the left (south) fork and proceed back to your starting point.

Next page: *You don't have to go far to enjoy the outdoors on Portland's east side (Hike 21).*

PORTLAND EAST

There is no shortage of opportunity to get outdoors for short or long trail-walking fixes in Portland's many east-side neighborhoods. This is just one of the area's many highlights that keeps locals close to home. Here, amid the city's melting pot of eclectic coffee shops, gourmet ice cream parlors, organic grocery stores, movie theater pubs, neighborhood farmers markets, corner dive bars, and every international flavor you could possibly have a craving for, are a number of prominent, forested buttes that create the hubs of the surrounding communities. These forested mounds—most featuring extensive trail networks—are all ancient volcanoes associated with the Boring volcanic formation, which shaped much of the region between Mount Hood and the Willamette River.

Fortunately for locals and visitors alike, this region offers more than forested hills, making the trail and walking menu as extensive as the area's dining menu. You can take a walk along an urban waterfront, through a historic cemetery (which is also the city's second-largest arboretum), around a recovering wetland, or through a tranquil flower garden—all while sipping organic, fair-trade coffee or licking a cone of strawberry-honey-balsamic-black-pepper ice cream. And to top off the appeal of Portland's east side, most of the parks and trail destinations are easily accessible using public transit or bike routes.

18

Tom McCall
Waterfront Park

DISTANCE:	4.4-mile loop
ELEVATION GAIN:	Up to 210 feet
HIGH POINT:	40 feet
DIFFICULTY:	Easy
FITNESS:	Walkers, runners, cyclists, barrier-free
FAMILY-FRIENDLY:	Suitable for all ages
DOG-FRIENDLY:	Leashed
BIKE-FRIENDLY:	Permitted
AMENITIES:	Parks, museums, food and drinks, arts and crafts, restrooms, historic bridges, river views
MANAGEMENT:	Portland Parks and Recreation
GPS:	N 45° 30.354', W 122° 39.870'
OTHER:	Amenity hours vary by day and season. There are numerous events that happen along the waterfront in spring and summer months, including the Cinco de Mayo Fiesta, Portland Pride Festival, Portland Rose Festival, Waterfront Blues Festival, and Oregon Brewers Festival. Visit www.travelportland.com and search the events calendar for more info.

GETTING THERE

Transit: Take TriMet bus 9 or 17 to Tilikum Crossing. Or take the MAX Orange Line from the Milwaukie area, or the Portland Streetcar, which both have stops right near the bridge at OMSI/SE Water Avenue.

Driving: Head for OMSI on SE Water Avenue, between SE Division and Clay Streets. Find free street parking in the area. Walk a few minutes to Tilikum Crossing bridge to begin.

Bike: From southeast neighborhoods, ride the Clinton Street bike route west to Tilikum Crossing; from northeast and downtown areas, ride the Eastbank Esplanade south to the bridge.

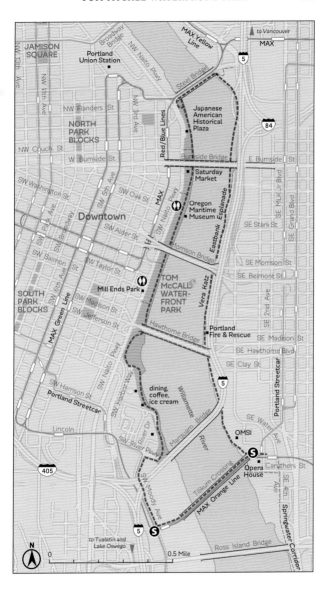

Tilikum Crossing, the Bridge of the People

The Willamette waterfront, while less of a hike and more of a paved stroll, is too good to be missed. With its abundance of eateries, sights, parks, and seasonal attractions and events, it's easy to walk, run, or ride this loop while also fetching your morning coffee, picking up a quirky gift for your aunt, or showing visitors some of what makes Portland so great. And the people-watching around here is usually fabulous—watch out for a variety of buskers, artists, and Portland's famed unicycle-riding, bagpipe-playing Darth Vader! And with a total of four bridges that you can cross back and forth, you can customize your outing to fit the time you have available.

GET MOVING

Start your stroll near the Portland Opera House and cross Portland's newest bridge: Tilikum Crossing, the Bridge of the People. (*Tilikum* is Chinook for "people.") Opened in 2015 as a pedestrian and public transit crossing, this modern cable-stayed bridge employs an artistic lighting system that responds to the Willamette's water speed, depth, and temperature. Once you reach the west side, turn right (north) on SW Moody Avenue and continue 0.3 mile to SW River Parkway. Continue straight through the condo buildings to South Waterfront Park. Hop on the pedestrian path and begin ambling north. Here you will find several cafés, coffee shops, and an ice cream parlor to help satisfy any breakfast, lunch, or snack cravings.

Continue by crossing the large grassy amphitheater that hosts the summer Waterfront Blues Festival and proceed on the wide paved path under the Hawthorne Bridge. (This is your first option for a shorter loop.) Now take a leisurely stroll along the Willamette and enjoy your company. If you walk across the grass to the intersection of SW Naito Parkway and SW Taylor Street, you can see Mill Ends Park, a tiny planter box with the unique designation as the world's smallest park. Proceed along Waterfront Park and under the Morrison Bridge. Bring snacks and a blanket for a picnic, or toss a Frisbee around with your pooch. If you're up for some Northwest history, visit the Oregon Maritime Museum on a steam-powered sternwheeler. (Visit oregonmaritimemuseum .org for tour times.)

Just south of the Burnside Bridge (your next option for a shorter loop), at 2 miles, is Portland's famous Saturday Market—which is actually open Saturdays and Sundays in season (www.portlandsaturdaymarket.com). Here, you can find just the right piece of Portlandia for whoever may be on your gift list. Browse among artisans showcasing pottery, jewelry, apparel, and a variety of creative Northwest arts and crafts. Hungry again? Pull up to one of the many food trucks parked nearby and indulge in some of the tastes that have made Portland a mecca of the food-truck phenomenon. After your visit to the market, pass under the Burnside Bridge to the Japanese American Historical Plaza and its row of cherry trees that bloom spectacularly in the springtime.

Start on the return trip by crossing the Steel Bridge to the east side of the Willamette and turn south. The path dips down to water level at the Vera Katz Eastbank Esplanade on a floating walkway popular with anglers. The path then rises back up above the river to continue southward, passing familiar bridges as it parallels I-5 above. Back near the Hawthorne Bridge, at 3.6 miles, pass Portland Fire and Rescue Station 21, then continue under I-5's Marquam Bridge to OMSI (Oregon Museum of Science and Industry). Here you can check out science exhibits, conduct your own experiments in one of the many science labs (a favorite with kids), catch a presentation at the Empirical Theater or planetarium, or tour a World War II submarine. When you've done all you can, return to your starting point, which is just a few minutes' walk away.

19   Lone Fir Cemetery

DISTANCE:	1.3 miles of paths
ELEVATION GAIN:	Up to 80 feet
HIGH POINT:	160 feet
DIFFICULTY:	Easy
FITNESS:	Walkers, barrier-free
FAMILY-FRIENDLY:	Suitable for all ages
DOG-FRIENDLY:	Not permitted
BIKE-FRIENDLY:	Not permitted
AMENITIES:	Street parking, historical info
MANAGEMENT:	Oregon Metro
GPS:	N 45° 31.086', W 122° 38.352'

OTHER: Cemetery open dawn to dusk. The Friends of Lone
           Fir Cemetery offer epitaph and historical walking
           tours on the first and second Saturday of each
           month, as well as the hauntingly fantastic Tour of
           Untimely Departures every year around Halloween;
           visit their website for more info.

GETTING THERE

Transit: TriMet bus 15 westbound stops on SE Morrison Street at SE 26th Avenue. Bus 15 eastbound stops on SE Belmont Street at SE 26th; walk one block north to the cemetery.

Driving: The Lone Fir Cemetery is located in Southeast Portland, between SE Stark and SE Morrison Streets, and between SE 20th and SE 26th Avenues. The main entrance and street parking are located on SE 26th Avenue.

Bike: Use the designated bike routes on SE Salmon Street (south of the cemetery) or SE Ankeny Street (north of the cemetery) to ride to the entrance on SE 26th Avenue.

Unless you live in the neighborhood, there's something most locals don't even realize: the city's oldest pioneer cemetery is located right in the heart of Southeast Portland. The first permanent resident of the burial ground, which was on private land at the time and later became the Mount Crawford Cemetery, was Emmor Stephens, who was buried in 1846. This was before the expansion of Portland, when the land east of the Willamette River was still rural farm country. In 1866, the cemetery was sold and its name changed to Lone Fir, for the single fir tree that grew on the property at the time.

Today, what was once a barren parcel with a solitary tree is now Portland's second-largest arboretum. In addition to its deceased residents, the cemetery is home to more than five hundred trees of seventy different species, which, in turn, are home to more than ninety bird species. Intermingled with the weathered and mossy tombs and headstones, the cemetery includes memorials to soldiers of America's early wars and Portland's firefighters, a Scottish mausoleum, a large Celtic cross, several obelisks, and the Pioneer Rose Garden. The site will soon add a Cultural Heritage Garden to memorialize some of Portland's early immigrant communities.

GET MOVING

Cemetery visitors are invited to take a trip back in time and examine the gravestones, monuments, and markers on 1.3 miles of flat paved paths. There isn't one recommended route around the cemetery; just explore at your leisure. There are benches for sitting at some locations and a few interpretive signs detailing some of the more significant markers. As you wander under the trees and survey the aging, weathered monuments, please be respectful of the peace of this location by keeping small children under control and noise to a minimum.

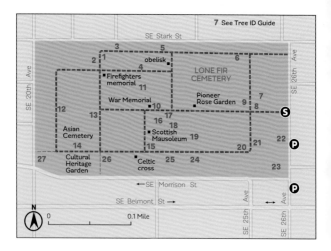

LONE FIR CEMETERY TREE GUIDE

What started as a barren plot with a single fir tree has since turned into one of Portland's finest tree gardens. As you stroll among the silent, weathering graves, use this key to help you identify some of the various tree species.

Portland's oldest cemetery is also its second-largest arboretum.

1. The original Lone Fir*
2. Ginkgo
3. Sitka spruce
4. Western hemlock
5. Incense cedar*
6. European beech
7. Grand fir
8. Weeping willow
9. English holly
10. Tulip tree
11. Giant sequoia
12. Red horse chestnut
13. Western red cedar
14. Flowering cherry
15. Oregon white oak
16. Eastern white pine
17. General Lane big-leaf maple*
18. American chestnut
19. Eucalyptus
20. Western red cedar
21. Southern magnolia
22. Port Orford cedar
23. Big-leaf maple
24. Young's weeping birch
25. Pacific yew
26. Flowering dogwood
27. Oregon ash

* Portland Heritage Tree. These are trees designated by the city for their unique size, age, historical, or horticultural significance. There are nearly three hundred heritage trees in the Portland area.

FROM THE NOTABLE TO THE NOTORIOUS

Lone Fir Cemetery has a storied and colorful past and hosts a who's who of Portland's early settlers. The residents range from judges and governors to acrobats and prostitutes. There are also a large number of asylum patients and Chinese immigrants interred at Lone Fir. Among the notable residents are Asa Lovejoy, a cofounder of Portland who preferred the name Boston over Portland; George Himes, founder of the Oregon Historical Society; and Charity Lamb, who murdered her abusive husband with an ax and was committed until her death.

20 Laurelhurst Park

DISTANCE:	2.2 miles of paths
ELEVATION GAIN:	Up to 130 feet
HIGH POINT:	90 feet
DIFFICULTY:	Easy
FITNESS:	Walkers, runners, cyclists, some barrier-free
FAMILY-FRIENDLY:	Suitable for all ages
DOG-FRIENDLY:	Permitted; off-leash area
BIKE-FRIENDLY:	Permitted
AMENITIES:	Restrooms, picnic areas, horseshoe pits, playground, sports court
MANAGEMENT:	Portland Parks and Recreation
GPS:	N 45° 31.308', W 122° 37.386'
OTHER:	Park hours 5:00 AM to 10:30 PM

GETTING THERE

Transit: TriMet bus 75 makes several stops on SE Cesar E. Chavez Boulevard near the park.

Driving: Laurelhurst Park is located in Southeast Portland, between SE Ankeny and SE Oak Streets, and between SE 33rd Avenue and SE Cesar E. Chavez Boulevard. Find street parking on Ankeny and Oak; park entrances can be found on all sides.

Bike: Use the designated bike routes on SE Ankeny Street or SE 45th Avenue to reach the park.

Portland takes great pride in its community parks and green spaces—especially when there's some historical significance to them. In the case of Laurelhurst Park, it began as Hazel Fern Farm, a grazing parcel and watering hole for cattle, then owned by William S. Ladd, Portland's two-time mayor in the 1850s and developer of Ladd's Addition. In 1911, the City of Portland bought thirty acres of the farm to turn into a community park and employed the Olmsted Brothers to develop it using their natural landscaping aesthetic. In 1919, Laurelhurst Park was awarded the most beautiful park on the West Coast by the Pacific Coast Parks Association. Today, nestled among charming cottages, Tudors, and bungalows, Laurelhurst Park is still one of the gems of Southeast Portland.

GET MOVING

There's no one way to stroll around Laurelhurst Park. From whichever side you enter, you can just wander at will among

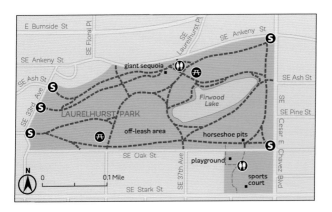

Springtime brings colorful blooms of camelias and hellebores to Laurelhurst Park.

the park's 2.2 miles of mostly paved paths. The main perimeter trail skirts most of the park's features and amenities, largely under a prolific canopy of deciduous and evergreen trees. The majority of these trees are Douglas and grand firs, western red cedars, and western red oaks. These are accompanied by an assortment of pine, spruce, cherry, yew, ash, hemlock, linden, hawthorn, beech, dogwood, plum, and even a giant sequoia. Check out the park's tree map at the kiosk near the lake to help you identify them.

On the north side of the park, the path contours Rhododendron Hill, where large shrubs bloom in a kaleidoscope of color in the spring months. This is where you can admire the park's giant sequoia, which vaults toward the heavens. Near the west end of the park, a dirt path branches off the main trail and contours the hillside back to the central area. The slope through here is decorated with more flowering shrubs, including magnolias, chocolate lilies, and morning glories. To make a full loop, exit the park at SE 33rd Avenue, turn left (south), and reenter the park before reaching SE Oak Street.

On the south side of the park, the main path forks near the west boundary, with one route sticking to the perimeter and the other heading into the park's interior. Near the center of the park, the path passes the large off-leash area where plenty of pooches get to roam and play freely. (Check the Parks and Recreation website for off-leash hours.) Near the east end, the path passes a range of horseshoe pits, then curves around to connect with the park's interior lake loop and the north-side perimeter path.

At the center of the park, an open, grassy meadow is a nice place to toss a ball or Frisbee, with plenty of picnic tables nearby. Here, a shorter, 0.4-mile paved path circles Firwood Lake, a three-acre spring-fed pool that fills the east side of the park, where ducks and geese can often be seen paddling about. The several picnic areas within the park are able to accommodate large and small groups, and several well-placed benches allow you to just kick back and watch the breeze rustle the trees.

21 Mount Tabor Park

DISTANCE:	12.5 miles of paths, trails, and roads
ELEVATION GAIN:	Up to 340 feet
HIGH POINT:	640 feet
DIFFICULTY:	Easy to challenging
FITNESS:	Walkers, hikers, runners, cyclists, some barrier-free
FAMILY-FRIENDLY:	Suitable for all ages; some steep trails; roads often used by bikers and skaters
DOG-FRIENDLY:	Permitted; off-leash area
BIKE-FRIENDLY:	Permitted on most trails; refer to park map

AMENITIES:	Parking, info, picnic tables, playground, tennis courts, amphitheater, restrooms, viewpoint
MANAGEMENT:	Portland Parks and Recreation
GPS:	N 45° 30.930', W 122° 35.796'
OTHER:	Park hours 5:00 AM to midnight; parking area 5:00 AM to 10:00 PM. Every summer Mount Tabor hosts free Concerts in the Park, and the Portland Adult Soapbox Derby, a fun event for all ages; for the latter, visit www.soapboxracer.com for event dates and info.

GETTING THERE

Transit: TriMet bus 15 makes several stops on SE Yamhill and SE Belmont Streets, just a few blocks from the north entrance. Bus 4 makes several stops on SE Division Street, south of the park, between SE 60th and SE 71st, each about a ten-minute walk from the park. Bus 71 has two stops on the southwest side of the park on SE 60th.

Driving: The main parking area on the north side of the park can be accessed via SE Stark Street and SE 69th Avenue. From this intersection, head south on 69th for 0.3 mile. Turn right (west) on SE Salmon Way for 0.2 mile to the parking area and trailheads. There is also parking on the road shoulders on the northwest side on SE Salmon Street, off SE 60th Avenue, and on the southeast side on SE Harrison Drive, off SE 72nd Avenue.

Bike: The park can be accessed via SE 69th on the north side, SE Harrison on the east side, SE Lincoln on the southwest side, and SE Salmon Way/Reservoir Loop Drive on the northwest side. Some trails in the park are closed to bicycles.

With more than a dozen miles of hiking trails, paved paths, and shared roadways, you can easily tailor an outing on Mount Tabor for as long or short as you like. With all these intertwining routes, and few visual references to the wider world, it's easy to lose your bearings. If you're new to the area or trying out Mount Tabor for the first time, pick up a trail map at the information booth (or download and print one before you go), and

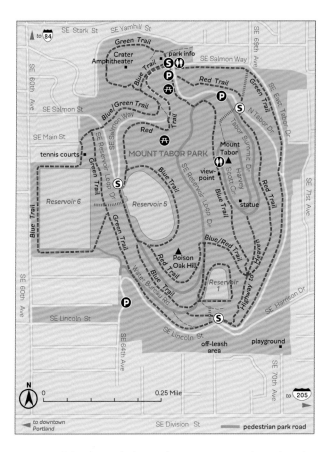

try one of the three designated routes to get oriented to the park. All three of these trails start on the north side near the information booth near the parking lot and amphitheater. You can also get flower and tree guides to help you identify much of the park's flora you may find as you roam.

GET MOVING

The 1-mile **Red Trail** is a nice introduction to the park. It makes an undulating circuit around the butte's forested middle on the

A rare blanket of snow on Portland's Mount Tabor

east side, then presents a nice view over the downtown area and Portland's West Hills. Head east on well-graded trail, climb the stairs to cross North Tabor Drive, then veer left (southeast) back onto dirt trail. Gain a little elevation as you contour around the hill, paralleling Tabor Summit Drive. Turn left at a posted junction and continue south to a wide junction with the Blue Trail. Proceed west downhill, cross Reservoir Loop Drive, then veer left to circuit Poison Oak Hill. When the trail spills onto Reservoir Loop Drive, walk the road past the reservoir to a gate, then veer right (north) and follow a narrow trail that parallels SE Salmon Way. Complete the loop by circuiting around the Crater Amphitheater and returning to your starting point.

For a more moderate hike, try the 1.7-mile **Green Trail**. This route sticks to the mountain's lower forested areas and utilizes a combination of roads and walking paths. Start by walking east on SE Salmon Way, then south on SE East Tabor Drive, gaining a little elevation to the fork with N. Tabor Drive. Continue south on the road, now descending, and try to spy Mount Hood to the east. Where the road turns west, proceed through a gate, pass a stairway, and veer right up into the trees on a dirt trail. Gain a little more elevation, cross Water Bureau Road, then traverse the shrubby hillside between Mount Tabor's two largest reservoirs. The trail wraps around the tennis courts to a sharp switchback, which makes a moderate ascent to the northeast. Follow this pathway as it parallels below SE Salmon Way, dips through a swale, then circuits around the amphitheater and back to your starting point.

The longest marked loop on Mount Tabor is the 3-mile **Blue Trail**. This route is best taken counterclockwise and has a few good ascents and stair climbs to get your daily cardio. Start with a quick circuit around the amphitheater, then head south, paralleling SE Salmon Way. Descend west, cross the lower road, and proceed around the tennis courts. Now follow a paved path to circuit Reservoir no. 6, then head for the stairs on the east side of the reservoir. Climb to Reservoir no. 5 and make a clockwise circuit on either the paved path or the paralleling dirt trail. Hop across SE Reservoir Loop Drive to a dirt path and head south, contouring around Poison Oak Hill, then make a loop around small Reservoir no. 1. Head up the side road back to Reservoir Loop Drive, then turn right (east) on a dirt trail and start ascending toward Mount Tabor's summit park and Harvey Scott Circle. Pick out views of Mounts Hood, St. Helens, and Adams on clear days. From the north end of the loop, descend on a wide duffy trail to the northwest, cross SE Reservoir Loop Drive one last time, then walk North Tabor Drive back to your starting point.

GO FARTHER

Once you've mastered the marked trails on Mount Tabor, it's time to create your own path. Mix and match some of the red, green, and blue sections with other trail sections. If you want a good, strenuous climb, try the Highway to Heaven trail, which climbs from the junction of SE Lincoln Street and SE Harrison Drive to the summit loop. As the mountain changes through the seasons—spring blooms, summer sun, fall color, and even winter snow (great for snowshoeing!)—it makes this unassuming urban peak a year-round outdoor hot spot.

22 Crystal Springs Rhododendron Garden

DISTANCE:	2 miles of paths
ELEVATION GAIN:	30 feet
HIGH POINT:	70 feet
DIFFICULTY:	Easy
FITNESS:	Walkers, barrier-free
FAMILY-FRIENDLY:	Suitable for all ages
DOG-FRIENDLY:	Leashed
BIKE-FRIENDLY:	Not permitted
AMENITIES:	Parking, restrooms, display gardens, interpretive tours, wedding site
MANAGEMENT:	Portland Parks and Recreation
GPS:	N 45° 28.794', W 122° 38.124'
OTHER:	Spring, summer hours 6:00 AM to 10:00 PM; fall, winter hours 6:00 AM to 6:00 PM; admission fee 10:00 AM to 6:00 PM, Wednesday through Sunday, March 1 through August 31; other days and times free; kids under twelve free year-round. The garden hosts several blooming events in April and May; it also hosts weddings. Visit their website for more info.

GETTING THERE

Transit: TriMet bus 19 makes stops near the corner of SE Woodstock Boulevard and SE 28th Avenue; walk north to the garden entrance. TriMet bus 10 makes stops near the corner of SE Steele Street and SE 28th Avenue; walk south to the garden entrance.

Driving: The garden is located on SE 28th Avenue, just north of SE Woodstock Boulevard and west of Reed College. From the southeast area, drive south on SE Cesar E. Chavez Boulevard to SE Woodstock Boulevard. Turn right for 0.6

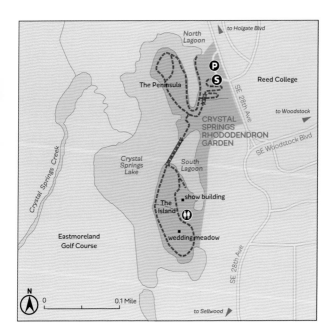

mile and proceed past the college. Veer right at the junction with SE 28th and go 0.1 mile to the garden entrance and parking area.

Bike: From the southeast area, ride SE 28th Avenue south to the garden.

Opened in 1950 as a test garden, Crystal Springs Rhododen-dron Garden occupies 9.5 acres of wooded city property on the east bank of spring-fed Crystal Springs Lake, just west of Reed College. The garden, managed by the City of Portland and maintained almost entirely by volunteers, showcases more than 2500 species of blooming plants. More than 2000 of these are rhodies, but there are also azaleas, hydrangeas, and other varieties on display, all under quiet, shady woods of Douglas fir, western red cedar, ginkgo, and vine maple.

A flower-lover's delight

Every spring, flower-peepers flock to Crystal Springs to wander among the vibrant blooms. Weekends in April and May see the most visitors, with crowds usually peaking on Mother's Day weekend—a good time *not* to visit the garden. Avoid the crowds during this period by visiting the park early in the morning, or in the evening. Better yet, visit during the off-season, when many things are still blooming, but the park is quiet, allowing you to stroll casually and unimpeded. A walk around the garden is a great way to unwind after work.

GET MOVING

Begin your stroll by proceeding through the entrance structure to stand under a massive blue atlas cedar. This stately *Cedrus* predates the garden, and the path that continues inside was actually built around the tree in order to leave it in place. From this initial vantage point, you get an overview of the garden: paved and gravel paths, bridges, ponds, waterfalls, and—during blooming season—more flowers than there are stars in the night sky. (Or so it seems.) Proceed into the garden, either by crossing the bridge or by descending to the first of several decorative waterfalls, then walk around to the North Lagoon. As you roam, you will find each plant marked with a species plaque or number. (Unfortunately, at this time, the garden does not provide any information to help you identify these.)

Since there's not far to go, just amble at will. There are two main areas to explore: the Peninsula and the Island, separated by a bridge between Crystal Springs Lake and South Lagoon. Both sections are crisscrossed with numerous paths that separate the various species pads. Interspersed around the garden are plenty of benches for sitting and admiring the trees, flowers, lagoons, and lake. Mallard, wood, and ruddy ducks and Canada geese are common residents of the garden's waters, but there are more to be seen. Keep your eyes peeled for herons, kinglets, scaups, chickadees, buffleheads, and even bald eagles. These are just a few of the more than ninety bird species often seen in and around the garden. Unrushed, just enjoy wandering the verdant, tranquil grounds.

23 Oaks Bottom Wildlife Refuge

DISTANCE:	2.8 miles roundtrip
ELEVATION GAIN:	120 feet
HIGH POINT:	90 feet
DIFFICULTY:	Easy
FITNESS:	Walkers, runners, cyclists, some barrier-free
FAMILY-FRIENDLY:	Suitable for all ages
DOG-FRIENDLY:	Leashed
BIKE-FRIENDLY:	Permitted on North Woodlands, Springwater Corridor Trails; refer to park map
AMENITIES:	Parking, outhouse, interpretive signs
MANAGEMENT:	Portland Parks and Recreation
GPS:	N 45° 29.136', W 122° 39.000'
OTHER:	Park hours 5:00 AM to midnight; parking area 5:00 AM to 10:00 PM

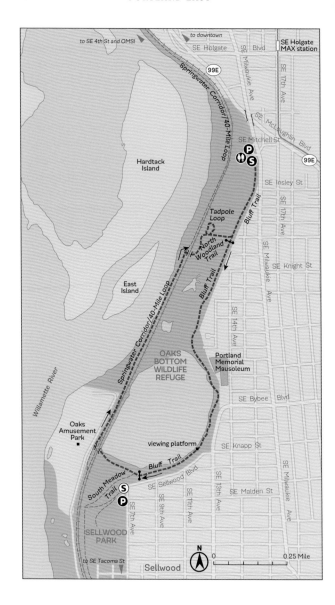

to SE 4th St and OMSI

to downtown

SE Holgate

SE Holgate

SE Blvd

SE Holgate
MAX station

99E

SE Milwaukie Ave

SE 17th Ave

Springwater Corridor/40-Mile Loop

SE McLaughlin Blvd

SE Mitchell St

99E

P
WC
S

Hardtack
Island

SE Insley St

SE 17th Ave

Bluff Trail

Tadpole
Loop

North
Woodland
Trail

SE Milwaukie Ave

SE Knight St

Bluff Trail

East
Island

SE 14th Ave

OAKS
BOTTOM
WILDLIFE
REFUGE

Portland
Memorial
Mausoleum

Springwater Corridor/40-Mile Loop

SE Bybee Blvd

Willamette River

Oaks
Amusement
Park

viewing platform

SE Knapp St

SE 13th Ave

SE Milwaukie Ave

Bluff Trail

South Meadow Trail

Sellwood Blvd

SE Malden St

S
P

SE 7th Ave

SE 9th Ave

SE 11th Ave

SELLWOOD
PARK

to SE Tacoma St

Sellwood

N

0   0.25 Mile

GETTING THERE

Transit: North trailhead: TriMet bus 19 makes a stop right near the trailhead parking area; buses 30 and 70 also have stops nearby. The MAX Orange Line has a stop at SE 17th Avenue and SE Holgate Boulevard, about a ten-minute walk away. South trailhead: TriMet bus 99 stops at SE Tacoma Street and SE 7th Avenue, about a five-minute walk away.

Driving: North trailhead: From SE Powell Boulevard (US Highway 26), drive 1 mile south on SE Milwaukie Avenue (between SE 11th and 12th Avenues). Cross SE McLoughlin Boulevard (State Route 99E) and turn right into the refuge parking area. South trailhead: From SE Tacoma Street in Sellwood, drive 0.3 mile north on SE 7th Avenue and turn left into the parking area.

Bike: From the Springwater Corridor trailhead in the industrial area near OMSI (SE 4th Street and SE Division Avenue), ride 1 mile south on the Springwater Corridor to the refuge area.

Conveniently located near several Southeast Portland communities and easily accessible by car, bike, or public transit, Oaks Bottom makes for a pleasant location to get out for a stroll. In 1988, these wetlands—reclaimed from industrial development—were designated as Portland's first wildlife refuge. Here, you can walk along under Oregon white oaks, Pacific madrones, and black cottonwoods while keeping your eyes peeled for a variety of songbirds, raptors, waterfowl, and other wetland critters.

GET MOVING

Begin the 2.8-mile lollipop loop trail at the north parking area on SE Milwaukie Avenue. Proceed 0.25 mile down a paved path under shady trees, where chicory and Oregon grape adorn the trailside. There are several benches along the way that invite you to have a sit and watch for woodpeckers and hummingbirds flitting here and there. At the bottom of the

The wetlands at Oaks Bottom

hill, the path forks, with the North Woodland Trail (your return route) turning to the right (west) and the dirt Bluff Trail (foot-only) veering off to the left (south).

Continue on the Bluff Trail, and wind along under the trees, along the base of the hillside. You can spy the colorful mural painted on the outer walls of the century-old Portland Memorial Mausoleum just upslope. The 43,000-square-foot mural (one of the largest in the United States) depicts a variety of the birds that make the wetlands area their home. The menagerie includes a forty-foot osprey and a sixty-five-foot blue heron. The path proceeds over a series of boardwalks, where small springs spill out of the hillside and trickle down into the refuge's large pond. At the 1-mile mark, a large viewing platform offers wide views of the central wetlands. Birders are served well to have a pair of binoculars at this point.

Continue through the trees for another 0.3 mile until the path spills out into the open beside a wide, grassy clearing and the next fork in the road. Fork right (west) onto the South Meadow Trail, keeping the trees to your right and the clearing to your left. Near the 1.5-mile mark, the path passes under the railroad tracks and connects to the paved

Springwater Corridor; turn right (north) to continue your loop. Across the railroad tracks to your right (east) are wide views of the wetlands area; to your left is the (often) noisy Oaks Amusement Park.

Things quiet again as you leave the amusement park behind. Tall oaks line the side of the path on the left (west), with more views of the refuge to the right (east). Near 2.2 miles, the Springwater Corridor dips below the railroad tracks and the North Woodland Trail branches off to the right (east). Follow this graded path as it loops back into the refuge. Proceed to a side trail for the Tadpole Loop, a 0.1-mile path that circuits a tiny pond that's home to rare northern red-legged frogs. After your detour and frog-spotting, continue the final 0.1 mile east to return to the junction where you started the loop. Turn left (north) and proceed back up the hill to the parking area and your waiting vehicle or bus ride.

24 Powell Butte Nature Park

DISTANCE:	13.2 miles of paths and trails
ELEVATION GAIN:	Up to 580 feet
HIGH POINT:	630 feet
DIFFICULTY:	Easy to moderate
FITNESS:	Walkers, hikers, runners, cyclists, some barrier-free
FAMILY-FRIENDLY:	Suitable for all ages; some semi-steep trails; popular with mountain bikers
BIKE-FRIENDLY:	Permitted on most trails; refer to park map
DOG-FRIENDLY:	Not permitted
AMENITIES:	Parking, visitor center, restrooms, interpretive signs, viewpoints
MANAGEMENT:	Portland Parks and Recreation
GPS:	N 45° 29.430', W 122° 29.820'
OTHER:	Park hours 7:00 AM to 8:00 PM in spring and fall; 7:00 AM to 10:00 PM in summer; 7:00 AM to 6:00 PM in winter

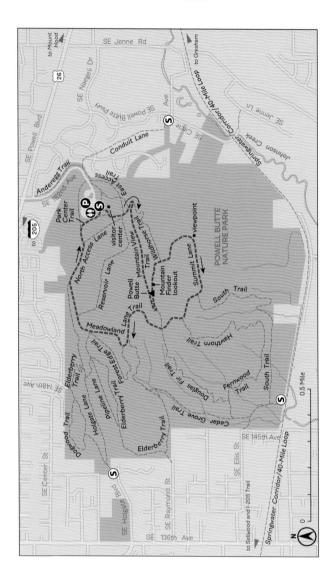

GETTING THERE

Transit: Take TriMet bus 9 to stops at SE 160th or SE 164th Avenues. Walk to SE 162nd Avenue and proceed south into park. Walk 0.5 mile up the Anderegg Trail to the visitor center.

Driving: From I-205 (exit 19) in Southeast Portland, take SE Powell Boulevard 3.4 miles east. Turn right on SE 162nd Avenue and continue 0.4 mile to the visitor center and parking turnaround at the road's end.

Bike: From the I-205 Trail south of SE Foster Road, ride the Springwater Corridor 2.8 miles east to the trailhead on the south side of the butte.

Situated atop and around an ancient lava dome, Powell Butte Nature Park offers year-round hiking, trail running, horseback riding, and mountain biking. Numerous trail-heads—including one on the Springwater Corridor cycling route—provide access to its network of more than 11 miles of trails and service roads, including a paved, barrier-free path to the viewpoint on the butte's summit. As you're wandering around this 612-acre natural area, you'd never guess that two 50-million-gallon reservoirs containing most of Portland's drinking water are right beneath your feet. Check out the interpretive displays at the visitor center to discover how engineers achieved this feat.

GET MOVING

For a pleasant outing with plenty of views, you can connect several trails for a 2.4-mile summit loop. From the visitor center, start on the paved Mountain View Trail. The path winds easily upward across the open summit plateau. In spring and summer, look for splashes of pearly everlasting and snow-berry along the trail and camas, lupine, and Oregon sunshine in the meadows. At the junction with the Summit Lane loop, turn left (east) and continue to the Mountain Finder lookout point at 0.7 mile. Here, several directional plaques help you identify many of the nearby peaks, including Mount Scott, Rocky Butte, Gresham Butte, and Larch Mountain, and a few of the farther peaks, including Mount St. Helens, Mount Adams, and Mount Jefferson.

With your elevation gain largely finished, continue the loop east, now on a gravel trail, where the way loops around groves of walnut and white oak. Before the trail turns at 1 mile, a short spur proceeds to a viewpoint with a stunning look at Mount Hood. The way now continues west along the preserve boundary area with several ponds below the trail; watch for deer, coyotes, skunks, and a variety of birds. Continue through the junctions with the South and Hawthorn Trails at 1.2 and 1.3 miles, respectively. At the four-way junction at 1.4 miles (where Summit Lane forks right and the Douglas Fir Trail forks left), continue straight ahead on the Meadowland Lane Trail. This portion curves through a couple more groves of oak trees and blackberry shrubs and passes the junctions with the 0.4-mile

There are plenty of paths for hikers, bikers, and runners at Powell Butte.

Forest Edge Trail side loop, which is a pleasant little detour for a change of scenery.

Nearing 1.9 miles, the Meadowland Trail ends at a T-junction with the Pipeline Lane road. Veer right (north) onto this dirt road and continue to where the road forks beside a maintenance building. Veer left (east) onto North Access Lane for a short spell, then right (south) onto the gravel Park Center Trail. The final stretch of the loop passes the park residence building, then ends at the visitor center.

GO FARTHER

There are plenty of opportunities for adding mileage to your hike and exploring some of the butte's forested west flanks, including a nearly century-old walnut grove. From the summit loop, veer onto the 0.8-mile South Trail or Hawthorn Trail. Use the short Fernwood Trail connector from the Hawthorn Trail and return via the 0.6-mile Douglas Fir Trail, or connect the 0.4-mile Cedar Grove Trail with the 1.4-mile Elderberry Trail for a larger 4.3-mile loop. Or just mix and match a variety of trails to spend an entire day wandering all over.

RIDE IT

Head out to Powell Butte via the Springwater Corridor and enter the park via a short spur trail. Veer left onto the Cedar Grove Trail for an easy ride through the forest. Turn right onto the Elderberry Trail and grind 0.3 mile uphill to the Meadowland Lane Trail. For a shorter, 2.6-mile loop, turn right, then left onto the Summit Lane Loop and enjoy the wide views. Turn left again on the South Trail and rip down through the forest back to your starting point. For a longer, 3.8-mile loop, turn left on Meadowland Lane and ride the Pipeline Lane road to the Mountain View Trail to the Summit Lane Loop. Finish the same as the shorter loop by proceeding down the South Trail. Bikes are not permitted on the Hawthorn, Wildhorse, and Reservoir Lane Trails.

25 Mount Talbert Nature Park

DISTANCE:	3.9 miles of trails
ELEVATION GAIN:	Up to 600 feet
HIGH POINT:	590 feet
DIFFICULTY:	Moderate
FITNESS:	Walkers, hikers, runners
FAMILY-FRIENDLY:	Suitable for older children; be aware of poison oak
DOG-FRIENDLY:	Not permitted
BIKE-FRIENDLY:	Not permitted
AMENITIES:	Parking, restrooms, picnic tables, interpretive signs
MANAGEMENT:	Oregon Metro
GPS:	N 45° 25.230', W 122° 33.156'
OTHER:	Park hours sunrise to sunset

GETTING THERE

Transit: Use TriMet bus 155. The northern trailhead is across the street from the SE 117th Avenue bus stop.

Driving: From I-205 (exit 14) in Happy Valley, drive east on SE Sunnybrook Boulevard to the stoplight at SE 97th Avenue. Turn right and continue 0.8 mile. The road curves left at SE Mather Road; continue another 0.2 mile. Turn left into the park's parking area; the trailhead is near the restrooms.

Mount Talbert is a forested butte in Happy Valley surrounded by a residential area and just east of I-205 and the Clackamas Town Center. The main Park Loop Trail winds and undulates around the hill under the cover of a variety of evergreen and deciduous trees, with ferns, berries, and seasonal shrubs adorning the trailside. With multiple trailheads and easy access, it's a great location for a casual stroll or invigorating run in the forest before or after work or school—where you may even spy some of its resident wildlife—without having to leave the city. Due to the sensitive

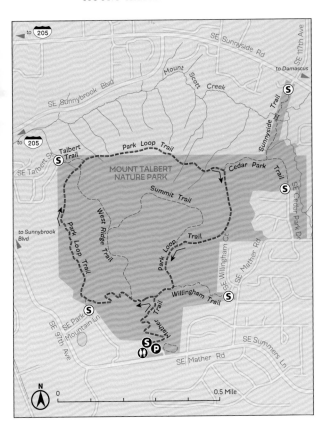

nature of this park, dogs are not permitted. And be on the lookout for poison oak.

GET MOVING

For the 2.3-mile loop around the mountain, start at the SE Mather Road trailhead and begin with a moderate, 0.3-mile ascent to connect with the Park Loop Trail. At the junction, turn left (west) to begin your clockwise loop. The trail proceeds along a fairly level grade to the junction with the West Ridge

Oak groves on Mount Talbert

Trail (see Go Farther) at 0.3 mile. The route then descends as it curves around the west side of the park. Notice how the flora begins as white oaks and berry bushes on the sunnier south slopes and transitions to ferns and Douglas firs on the shadier north slopes. At 1 mile, the loop route passes the northern junction with the West Ridge Trail, quickly after which it meets the Talbert Trail, a 0.1-mile spur to a trailhead at the end of SE Talbert Street.

The loop continues, bending east, with a contouring ascent under shady conifers. The route comes to a crest at 1.3 miles on the north slope, then descends quickly to the next trail-head junction in a shallow draw at just under 1.5 miles. Here, a spur trail descends quickly for 0.2 mile to a fork, where the left (north) fork continues down another 0.2 mile, crosses Mount Scott Creek, then ends at the trailhead near SE Sunnyside

Road; the right (east) fork gradually descends 0.1 mile to the trailhead at the end of SE Cedar Park Drive. Continuing past this spur-trail junction, the loop trail makes one more gentle ascent to a junction with the Summit Trail at 1.8 miles (see Go Farther).

The final stretch of the Park Loop Trail continues on an easy descent, curving south and passing the last of the trailhead junctions at 1.9 miles. To the left, a 0.2-mile spur descends on narrow tread to a little-used trailhead beside a home on SE Willingham Court. Continue to the right, just 0.1 mile farther to the junction where you started your journey. Turn left (south) and proceed back down to the trailhead and parking area on SE Mather Road.

GO FARTHER

Change up the scenery on repeat visits by incorporating the 0.5-mile West Ridge Trail or the 0.5-mile Summit Trail. The former cuts the west side of the Park Loop Trail short by staying high on the hillside and crossing a savanna of white oak trees, then descending through Douglas firs and ferns to reconnect with the Park Loop Trail on the opposite side; the latter branches off the West Ridge Trail and switchbacks moderately up through fern and snowberry, where you may spy rock outcrops giving hints of the butte's volcanic origins. From the viewless summit, it makes a quick descent to reconnect with the Park Loop Trail on the south side.

Next page: *From brushy savanna to lush forest, the Lake Oswego area has plenty to enjoy (Hike 29).*

LAKE OSWEGO

Immediately south of Portland's bustling metro area, and straddling the banks of the Willamette River, the communities of Lake Oswego, West Linn, and Oak Grove are known for their abundance of luxury homes and manicured lawns—quite a far departure from its 1850s roots as an industrial and mining town. It is also where you will find an abundance of nature parks and trail systems, which follows in the town's 1930s motto, "Live where you play." Today, this is good for helping the almost one hundred thousand area residents to get outdoors for some fresh air.

The centerpiece of the area's park system is 660-acre Tryon Creek State Natural Area (Hike 4), which was founded in 1975 following a twenty-five-year effort to preserve the wooded canyon. Located between the communities of Southeast Portland and the town of Lake Oswego, this should be one of your first visits in the area. Many of the area's other parks do well in preserving native flora and fauna, as well as showcasing the natural forces that shaped the region. This includes riparian woodlands, oak savannas, and volcanic plateaus.

26 Springbrook Park

DISTANCE:	2.1 miles of trails
ELEVATION GAIN:	Up to 130 feet
HIGH POINT:	430 feet
DIFFICULTY:	Easy
FITNESS:	Walkers, runners, some barrier-free
FAMILY-FRIENDLY:	Suitable for all ages
DOG-FRIENDLY:	Leashed
BIKE-FRIENDLY:	Permitted
AMENITIES:	Interpretive info, historical site
MANAGEMENT:	Lake Oswego Parks and Recreation
GPS:	N 45° 25.284', W 122° 42.438'
OTHER:	Park hours 6:00 AM to 10:00 PM

GETTING THERE

Transit: TriMet buses 37 and 38 stop at the corner of Boones Ferry Road and Rainbow Drive. Walk 100 yards east on Rainbow Drive, then 0.1 mile north on Diane Drive to the park entrance.

Driving: From the downtown area, drive approximately 7 miles south on I-5. Take exit 292 for Kruse Way; turn left (east) and continue 2.2 miles to Boones Ferry Road. Turn left (north) for 0.5 mile. Turn right (east) on Rainbow Drive, then an immediate left (north) on Diane Drive. Proceed to the park entrance at the end of the road; park on the street.

Bike: From Bridgeport Village, ride 2.8 miles northeast on Boones Ferry Road. Turn right (east) on Rainbow Drive, then an immediate left (north) on Diane Drive; proceed to the park entrance.

Since the early 1970s, Springbrook Park has provided the residents of, and visitors to, the Lake Oswego area the opportunity to get outdoors and stroll in the shade of a pleasant plot of hardwood forest. At fifty-two acres, and situated on

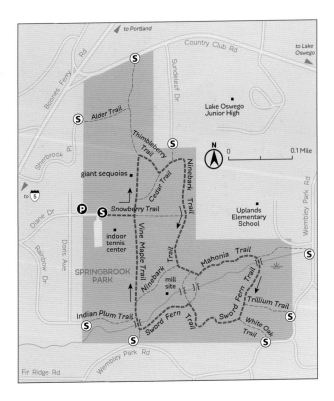

the northern flank of Iron Mountain, it is the community's largest park. Not only does the little pocket-woods provide a nice walking space, but its proximity to several schools gives local students an opportunity to learn about nature and forest recovery in a natural setting. But you don't have to be a student to appreciate these quiet woods, teeming with birds and small critters.

GET MOVING

To take in the entire park on a 1-mile, L-shaped loop, begin at the entrance at the end of Diane Drive and proceed 100 yards

Cherry blossoms in Springbrook Park

up the Snowberry Trail to a wide crossroads with the Vine Maple Trail. In springtime, cherry trees blossom in brilliant white blooms while overhead, tall big-leaf maples and red alders filter the sunlight onto swathes of trillium, bleeding heart, holly, and sword fern. A few stray Douglas firs and western red cedars add variety to the canopy. From this junction, you can pretty much just wander at will among several short interconnected loops. To continue on the 1-mile loop, turn left (north) and head up the Vine Maple Trail. Stay on this trail for a short distance, passing the Cedar Trail; the grove of trees to the left of the trail are giant sequoia.

When you reach the Thimbleberry Trail, veer right (southeast) and take this short spur 80 yards to another junction with the Cedar Trail. Veer left (northeast) another 80 yards to a wide junction with the Ninebark Trail. Here, the Cedar

Trail exits the park to Sundeleaf Drive, so turn right (east) and proceed along the boundary of the park near Lake Oswego Junior High. You can now enjoy strolling south for 0.2 mile, crossing the Snowberry Trail and meeting the Mahonia Trail. Now turn left (east) and enter the park's wetlands, where a couple of small creeks converge. Two trails branch off to the right (south) in quick succession. These lead to an old saw-mill site and a couple of small bridges that predate the park; explore at your leisure.

The Mahonia Trail exits the park through a student garden and onto the grounds of the Uplands Elementary School. Turn right (south) on the Sword Fern Trail and proceed through a swampy area of Oregon white oaks. The trail bends to the west, passing the Trillium and White Oak Trails, the two bridge trails, and meets the Vine Maple Trail. Close your loop by turning right (north) and proceeding past the Indian Plum and Ninebark Trails, which branch off to the left and right, respectively, and return to the junction where you started. If you've got the itch to wander more, do some backtracking and explore the portions of the Cedar, Snowberry, and Nine-bark Trails you skipped, or check out some of the short side spurs that exit the park.

27   Cooks Butte Park

DISTANCE:	2.5 miles of trails
ELEVATION GAIN:	400 feet
HIGH POINT:	720 feet
DIFFICULTY:	Moderate
FITNESS:	Walkers, hikers, runners
FAMILY-FRIENDLY:	Suitable for older children; some steep trails
DOG-FRIENDLY:	Leashed
BIKE-FRIENDLY:	Not permitted
AMENITIES:	Trailhead parking, interpretive info, benches

MANAGEMENT:	Lake Oswego Parks and Recreation
GPS:	N 45° 23.526', W 122° 41.622'
OTHER:	Park hours 7:00 AM to 10:00 PM

GETTING THERE

Transit: Not available.

Driving: From I-205 in Shadowood (between Tualatin and Oregon City), take exit 3 for SW Stafford Road. Turn right (north) and continue 1.8 miles. At the traffic circle at Rosemont Road, take the third exit onto Atherton Drive. Proceed 0.2 mile to the parking area at Stevens Meadows.

Bike: From Old Town in Lake Oswego, ride 0.8 mile southwest on McVey Avenue; continue another 1.1 miles on SW Stafford Road. At the Rosemont Road traffic circle, take the first exit onto Atherton Drive and proceed 0.2 mile to the trailhead.

Rising more than six hundred feet above the nearby Tualatin River, Cooks Butte is an extinct volcano now shrouded under a forty-two-acre canopy of mossy maple, alder, fir, and cedar forest. In springtime, among carpets of sword fern, licorice fern, and Oregon grape, the butte's shady slopes are covered with bright white trillium, yellow mountain violets, and little purple coast toothwort. The woodland here and nearby Stevens Meadows (see Go Farther) are good for bird-watching. Commonly viewed species include woodpeckers, wrens, juncos, flickers, hawks, osprey, and turkey vultures. With just 1.9 miles of interconnected trails, including a central 1.7-mile lollipop loop, this quiet wooded park can easily be explored in just a couple of hours.

GET MOVING

From the small parking area near the gate to Stevens Meadows (see Go Farther), walk west on the paved path. On the slope above are several high-end houses with enviable views over the meadows and river basin. At 0.2 mile, the trail

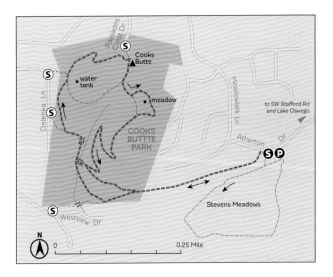

dips under forest cover and comes to the first junction just beyond. This is the start of your clockwise loop. The trail that branches off to the right (north) is your return route, so continue straight ahead (west) to the next junction at 0.3 mile. At this second junction, turn right (north) and begin a short, steady climb up the volcano's flank. The path that continues west leads to another trailhead at Westview Drive.

The grade eases around 0.5 mile and begins to contour the west slope of the butte. Here, a short spur trail branches off to the left (west) to Delenka Lane. After another short ascent, the trail ends at a gravel road junction beneath an old water storage tank; this is a common spot for raptors to perch while hunting for their next meal. Turn left (north) on the road, which quickly transitions back to a narrow hiking trail, and circuit the upper north slope of the butte through a stretch of dry, mossy debris to the next junction at 0.8 mile. To the left (north), the path proceeds to the park's upper trailhead at the end of Palisades Crest Drive; turn right (south) to continue your loop.

Now walk through the upper reaches of Cooks Butte, where little adorns the forest floor—a significant contrast from the lower slopes. Veer left (south) at a fork and come to the upper meadow junction at 0.9 mile. Veer left again and contour around the east side of the meadow; a few sparing views to the east can be had through pockets in the trees, and a bench offers a chance to sit and enjoy your surroundings. Where the meadow loop meets the main loop again, veer left (southwest) and begin descending the butte into increasingly dense and lush groundcover and wildflowers; along the way, the trail skirts a trickling spring in a verdant gully. Ignore the cutoff spur at the bottom of the third switchback and continue left (southeast) to close your loop at 1.5 miles. Turn left (east) at the junction to return to your starting point.

GO FARTHER

The 0.6-mile loop around Stevens Meadows doesn't add a ton of mileage to your outing, but it gives you the opportunity to circuit a pleasant open slope and watch for more

The meadow at Cooks Butte

birds and small critters. Proceed through the meadow gate near the parking area and start this loop counterclockwise by turning right (west) and walking along a grassy path. As you follow the circuit, the bottom of the loop dips into a low draw and crosses a planked boardwalk; blackberry shrubs line the bottom of the slope. Rounding the east side of the loop, the path climbs easily and offers a few more views, including that of the two lonely white oaks in the middle of the meadow. Before you know it, you're back at your starting point.

28 Mary S. Young State Recreation Area

DISTANCE:	5.7 miles of paths and trails
ELEVATION GAIN:	Up to 290 feet
HIGH POINT:	300 feet
DIFFICULTY:	Easy to moderate
FITNESS:	Walkers, hikers, runners, cyclists, some barrier-free
FAMILY-FRIENDLY:	Suitable for all ages; some open shoreline
DOG-FRIENDLY:	Permitted; off-leash area
BIKE-FRIENDLY:	On paved trails
AMENITIES:	Parking, restrooms, picnic sites, beach, sports fields
MANAGEMENT:	West Linn Parks and Recreation
GPS:	N 45° 22.848', W 122° 37.674'
OTHER:	Park hours 7:00 AM to sunset

GETTING THERE

Transit: TriMet bus 35 stops near the northwest and southwest corners of the park on Willamette Drive. Walk 0.2 mile south or north on the paved bike path to the Trillium Trail. Turn east into the park and proceed 0.7 mile to the main parking area.

Driving: From I-205 in West Linn, take exit 8 for Willamette Drive; turn north and drive 1.9 miles. Turn right into Mary S. Young State Recreation Area and proceed 0.6 mile to the main parking area.

Bike: Ride north or south along Willamette Drive; enter the park via the Trillium Trail.

Dedicated in 1972, Mary S. Young State Recreation Area is named for a prominent Lake Oswego citizen who was an active member of the local community in everything from the Garden Club to the Girl Scouts to the Civil Defense Corps. Between 1963 and 1966, Mary and her husband, Thomas, donated the land that is now named in her memory. Sadly, she passed away just a year before the park's completion and dedication. Located on the banks of the Willamette River, the park offers several miles of interconnected trails for exploring the area's forest and riverside. The two primary trails are the 0.6-mile Riverside Loop (with longer options) and the 1.6-mile Heron Creek Loop. The park also features sports fields and an off-leash dog recreation area.

Walk the banks of the Willamette River at Mary S. Young State Recreation Area.

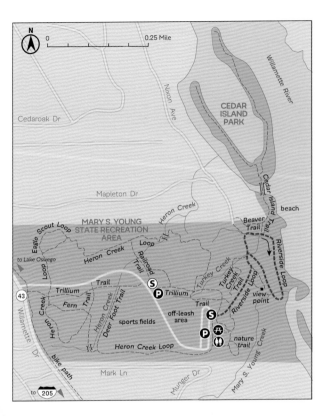

GET MOVING

Begin with an 0.6-mile walk to the Willamette River, where you may spy a variety of avians, waterfowl, and raptors. From the main parking area, proceed to the start of the Riverside Loop near the northeast corner. The wide paved path descends into shady Douglas fir and big-leaf maple forest; the route is lined with rhododendron, snowberry, thimbleberry, salal, and sword fern. Stay on the Riverside Loop path through several junctions, where other trails veer off to Turkey Creek and a viewpoint over Mary S. Young Creek;

explore these later at will. Just past where Turkey Creek runs under the path is a wide junction that begins the loop of the Riverside Loop; veer left (north) to begin a clockwise circuit. Make a short descent to another junction and turn right (east) then to yet another junction near where the pavement ends. To the left (north), the path proceeds to the banks of the Willamette River.

Here, you can veer off the main path for a look; watch for blackberries, morning glory, and jewelweed around the river-side. In the later spring and summer, you can cross a bridge onto Cedar Island for further exploring. Continue the loop by veering right (southeast) onto a dirt trail and proceeding through a grassy corridor between a row of cottonwoods and riverside shrubbery. The path eventually becomes paved again and hooks over Mary S. Young Creek. Follow this back to a familiar junction where you once again see Turkey Creek spilling under the path. Turn left (south) and head back to the parking area, or venture off and explore some of the connecting loop trails.

GO FARTHER

For a longer forested walk, try the 1.6-mile Heron Creek Loop. This loop is not well signed in some areas and has a lot of junctions, so you may want to carry a trail map with you. Begin at the northeast corner of the main parking area and plunge into the woods (east) on the Trillium Trail. Make two quick left turns to get on the Turkey Creek Trail and head in the opposite direction (west). In less than 0.2 mile, the Heron Creek Loop branches off to the right (north). The path meanders easily through the shaded forest; the way is lined with fringe cup, waterleaf, trillium, sword fern, and vine maple. Near 0.3 mile, the path dips to cross a small tributary, then dips again to cross Heron Creek. At 0.5 mile, the Railroad Trail branches off to the left (south).

Continue along the loop trail, where you now begin to encounter spots of yellow monkey flower and plenty of pink hedge nettle. Veer left (southwest) through the next two forks (these are for the Eagle Scout side loop), and bend south to cross the park's entrance road and the paved Trillium Trail around 0.9 mile. Turn right through the next two forks (southwest and south, respectively), looping through several stands of rhododendron, then cross a small bridge over Heron Creek at 1.2 miles. At the final junction, veer right to complete the loop by walking along the park's southern boundary under tall shade trees, passing alongside the sports fields, and return to the main parking area.

29 Camassia Natural Area

DISTANCE:	1.1 miles of trails
ELEVATION GAIN:	110 feet
HIGH POINT:	310 feet
DIFFICULTY:	Easy
FITNESS:	Walkers, runners
FAMILY-FRIENDLY:	Suitable for all ages; be aware of poison oak
DOG-FRIENDLY:	Not permitted
BIKE-FRIENDLY:	Not permitted
AMENITIES:	Parking, interpretive signs, viewpoints
MANAGEMENT:	Oregon Nature Conservancy
GPS:	N 45° 21.552', W 122° 37.092'
OTHER:	Park hours sunrise to sunset

GETTING THERE

Transit: TriMet bus 154 stops at the corner of Willamette Falls Drive and West A Street. From the bus stop, walk 0.5 mile to the natural area following the driving directions.

Driving: From I-205 in West Linn, take exit 8 for Willamette Drive. Turn south and veer right (southwest) on Willamette

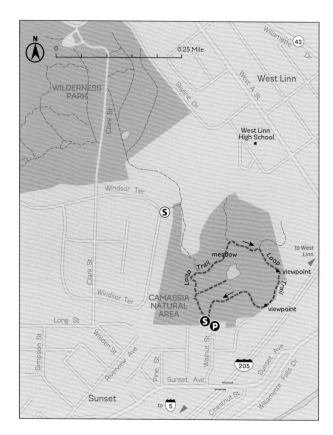

Falls Drive for another 0.3 mile. At the fork, veer right (west) onto Sunset Avenue and proceed just 0.2 mile. Turn right (north) on Walnut Street and proceed 0.1 mile to the trailhead at the end of the road.

Just a tiny pocket of a park, Camassia Natural Area is one of those hidden gems that even most locals aren't familiar with. Located high on a volcanic bluff above I-205 in West Linn, the twenty-six-acre natural area showcases an abundance of native flora—more than three hundred plant species, from lush coniferous forest and marshy wetlands to oak woodlands and grassy savannas—in addition to fascinating geologic formations that provide clues as to how this portion of the Willamette River valley was shaped. The area is also home to a variety of birds, mammals, and amphibians. Despite the main Loop Trail being less than 1 mile, you can easily spend hours exploring and observing all the interesting flora and fauna that make their home here.

GET MOVING

Head into the park through a split-rail gate. Just a few yards in, through thickets of Oregon grape and wild blackberry, the trail splits at a signboard. Pick up a copy of the park map and interpretive guide from the box. (Instead of discarding your brochure when you're finished, please return it to the box for future visitor use.) Begin your clockwise circuit by turning left (west). The path forward proceeds over alternating woodchip path and narrow, planked boardwalk. The surrounding brush—including sword fern, snowberry, false Solomon's seal, and little, stumpy stalks of purple flowers called self-heal—encroaches on the path in places. Watch out for stray blackberry vines reaching out to snag your socks and pant legs.

Continue forward to a signed junction. Here, a short path breaks off right (east) to the wetlands pond in the middle of the natural area; head in for a quick look where you may spot frogs, newts, and ducks. It can be a bit swampy and mucky, so watch your footing; proceed back to the loop and continue to the next signed junction. To the left (north), the path to Wilderness Park climbs easily to a small grassy meadow surrounded by white oaks. The path continues through overgrown snowberry to a trailhead on Windsor Terrace, then continues on to the park (see Go Farther). Turn right (east) to continue on the Loop Trail and proceed into the area's central savanna, which hosts a small grove of quaking aspen. In springtime, look

Wildflowers, oak, and aspen adorn the savanna at Camassia Natural Area.

for the purple blossoms of the park's namesake flower: the camas lily. You'll also find brodiaeas, blue-eyed Marys, fawn lilies, sea blush, and cow parsnip; watch out for poison oak. The pocked, rocky outcroppings are volcanic basalt.

Enjoy your stroll through the meadow, eventually turning back into the trees and bypassing a couple more side trails to stay on the main loop. On the east side of the loop, the trail briefly pops out of the trees to a viewpoint on a rocky bluff near a grove of madrones; the view looks over a wooded ravine. As the path continues circling around, it proceeds through a meadow restoration area where invasive plants are eradicated and replaced with native varieties, then it once again enters shadier Douglas fir forest adorned with Oregon grape and purple wooly vetch. Keep your eyes peeled for owls and woodpeckers in the trees. Before you get back to your starting point, you get one more view, where you can spot Mount Hood on clear days. Finish your loop back at the info board, then exit to the parking lot.

GO FARTHER

If you're in the mood for more exploring—highly likely since you can easily finish the natural area in less than an hour—take some time to go wander around fifty-one-acre Wilderness Park, with nearly two more miles of trails. From the signed junction on the northwest corner of the Loop Trail, veer left (north) and proceed 0.6 mile up the hill under Douglas fir and big-leaf maple forest into the park. When you reach Clark Street, cross and turn either direction to continue into the larger portion of the park where a network of short interconnected paths loop and wander around the wooded hillside. As you're strolling, look for wood violets, trillium, and candy flower among a variety of ferns, berries, salal, and vanilla leaf.

Next page: Discover natural wetlands, native prairie, and urban forest in Portland's backyard (Hike 32).

BEAVERTON

The towns of Beaverton, Tigard, and Tualatin lie west and south of Portland's downtown area and are home to more than 240,000 residents. The second-largest city in Washington County, Beaverton was established in the mid-1800s among the swamps and marshes of the Tualatin River floodplain. Fun fact: Beaverton's name is actually derived from the extensive number of beaver dams and ponds that used to occupy the area, as observed by early settlers. Steady development allowed the town and surrounding communities to grow and expand over the next century and a half, and in 2010, Beaverton was named "One of the best places to live," by *Money* magazine. No doubt, that quality of life is due, at least in part, to the area's 1400 acres of parks and natural areas—the largest parks district in the state.

Within those 1400 acres, locals and outdoor-lovers alike have more than ninety parks and natural areas to walk, hike, run, play, bike, ride horses, and watch wildlife—and this doesn't even count the area's easy access to the immense Forest Park or Tualatin River National Wildlife Refuge. Many of these parks are small and unassuming. Others, however, offer extensive path and trail networks for stretching your legs on morning jogs or after-work strolls—you're bound to find one nearby. Start with the Tualatin Hills Nature Park (Hike 3) in the Getting Acquainted section of this guide. This interpretive nature park will give you a background on the region's natural history, its settlement and development, and how those developers then realized the need to preserve natural areas for all to enjoy.

30 Orenco Woods Nature Park

DISTANCE:	1.5 miles of paths and trails
ELEVATION GAIN:	Up to 110 feet
HIGH POINT:	190 feet
DIFFICULTY:	Easy
FITNESS:	Walkers, runners, cyclists, some barrier-free
FAMILY-FRIENDLY:	Suitable for all ages
DOG-FRIENDLY:	Leashed; paved trails only
BIKE-FRIENDLY:	Paved trails only
AMENITIES:	Parking, restrooms, picnic area, nature play area, historic site, playground
MANAGEMENT:	Hillsboro Parks and Recreation
GPS:	N 45° 31.728', W 122° 54.408'
OTHER:	Park hours sunrise to sunset

GETTING THERE

Transit: Ride the MAX Blue Line west to the Orenco/NW 231st station. Walk east to NE Century Boulevard; turn right (south) and walk 0.1 mile to NE Birch Street. Turn left (east) and walk 0.4 mile to the park entrance.

  Driving: From the downtown area, drive US Highway 26 west approximately 11 miles to Tanasbourne. Take exit 62A for Cornelius Pass Road south; merge onto NE Cornelius Pass Road and continue 1.1 miles. Turn right (west) on NE Cornell Road for 0.7 mile, then left (south) on NE Century Boulevard for 0.4 mile. Turn left (east) on NE Birch Street and proceed 0.4 mile to the park entrance and parking area.

More than a century ago, the land occupied by the newly christened Orenco Woods Nature Park was owned by the Oregon Nursery Company, renowned for their Orenco apples. The historic McDonald House, built in 1912, is located on the park grounds and has been listed on the National Register of Historic Places. When the nursery shut down, the land served as a golf course for more than fifty years. When developers abandoned the land following the 2008 recession, the City of Hillsboro purchased the property in 2011 to renovate it into a park in order to preserve the riparian habitat and create more outdoor recreation space for local residents.

Open since 2017, this new forty-two-acre nature park is a community green space with a little something for everyone. It features a picnic area, playground, nature play area, grassy fields for exercising Fido, and nearly 2 miles of trails and walking paths that wind among the gentle knolls around Rock Creek and through groves of Douglas fir, big-leaf maple, and western red cedar. As the area has been given back to nature, wildlife has moved back in, making this a good spot to come animal-peeping. Watch for deer and beavers in the meadows and along the stream banks, and scan the trees for a variety of songbirds and raptors.

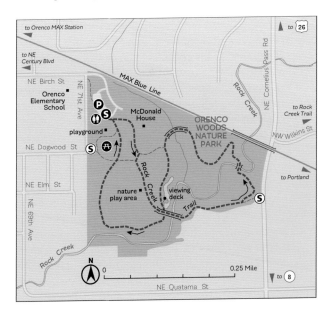

Orenco Woods' arched bridge

GET MOVING

The ideal way to explore the park is by making a 1.2-mile figure-eight loop. Start at the parking area and proceed east on a paved pathway toward the historic McDonald House. The house is not open to the public but can be viewed from outside. Follow the path south and merge onto the Rock Creek Trail. The route passes a grove of tall Douglas firs, under which a nature play area features several huge sculptures of fantastical forest beings that appear to be frozen in time. (Could they be Bilbo's trolls?) The path turns east again and crosses an impressive arched bridge over Rock Creek; below you will spy a large pond. The way continues through a corridor with the wooded creek bottom on your left and a housing development on your right. At 0.4 mile, just before the trail exits the park at NE Cornelius Pass Road, veer left (north) and dip into a shallow draw.

Now the path turns to a mix of gravel and wood chips and veers back into the park through a riparian area brimming with cow parsnip, red clover, Douglas spiraea, thistle, and dandelion. Cross two more bridges, the first over Rock Creek, and the next over a long curving trestle that spans a wooded basin. Bending south, head for the arched bridge you crossed earlier. Just before proceeding underneath, a short path juts off left (east) to a viewing deck next to the pond you spied from above. Pop over for a quick peek and see if any of the local residents are home. The final stretch curves gently upward through more Douglas firs, alder, and hawthorn, then reenters the main park area. Close your loop by proceeding along a line of tall white oaks, past the picnic shelter and playground, and return to your starting point.

GO FARTHER

Add more mileage to your walk or ride by taking a 2-mile (one-way) stroll up the Rock Creek Trail. The path proceeds along Rock Creek, through Orchard Park and past woodlands and open meadows. Find the trail by exiting the east side of Orenco Woods Nature Park and crossing NE Cornelius Pass Road. Turn left (north) and walk 0.1 mile to NW Wilkins Street; turn right (east) and proceed 0.2 mile to the trailhead on the north side of the road near a large sign. Head up the trail, wandering as far as you like. The path ends at NW Rock Creek Boulevard, just north of US 26. Backtrack to your starting point.

31 Cooper Mountain Nature Park

DISTANCE:	3.8 miles of trails
ELEVATION GAIN:	Up to 390 feet
HIGH POINT:	770 feet
DIFFICULTY:	Easy to moderate
FITNESS:	Walkers, hikers, runners, some barrier-free
FAMILY-FRIENDLY:	Suitable for all ages; some steep trails

DOG-FRIENDLY:	Not permitted
BIKE-FRIENDLY:	Not permitted
AMENITIES:	Parking, nature center, restrooms, interpretive signs, playground, viewpoint, demonstration garden
MANAGEMENT:	Tualatin Hills Parks and Recreation
GPS:	N 45° 27.156', W 122° 52.212'
OTHER:	Park hours sunrise to sunset. The Cooper Mountain Nature House offers year-round guided walks, kids camps, and nature programs for all ages. Visit the wesite for more info and a calendar of events.

GETTING THERE

Transit: Not available.

Driving: From State Route 217 in Tigard, use exit 4B for SW Scholls Ferry Road and Washington Square. At the bottom of the ramp, turn left (south) onto Scholls Ferry and proceed 2.4 miles to SW Murray Boulevard; turn right (north) and continue 0.6 mile. Turn left (west) on SW Weir Road for another 1.2 miles, then right on SW 170th Avenue for 0.2 mile. Turn left on SW Kemmer Road and proceed 1 mile to the park entrance on the left (south).

Home to one of the last remaining plots of native upland prairie, Cooper Mountain Nature Park offers a small glimpse of the kind of wide oak savannas that used to cover the slopes surrounding the Tualatin River valley. Here, the park management even practices prescribed burns and other techniques in the same way that the native peoples did in order to preserve and maintain the prairie in its original form. Within the park, more than two hundred species of birds, mammals, amphibians, and reptiles make their homes, and every spring, the meadows erupt in dramatic and colorful carpets of wildflowers. A central, 2.1-mile loop trail explores the Big Prairie and surrounding woodlands, while a shorter side loop—great for smaller children—visits the Little Prairie. Bird-watchers will find unusual varieties inhabiting the trees and grasslands throughout the year.

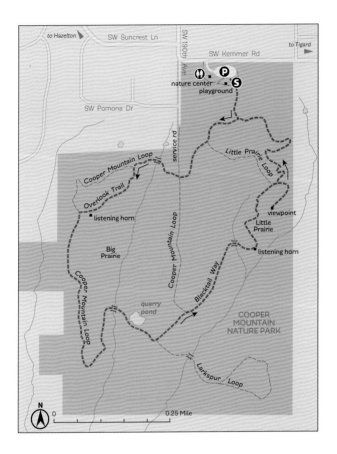

GET MOVING

Near the southeast corner of the parking area, start on the Little Prairie Loop by heading down a wide graded path that gently descends a grassy slope adorned with Queen Anne's lace and young ponderosa pines. At 0.1 mile the path forks, with the 0.6-mile Little Prairie Loop veering left (east) and the Cooper Mountain Loop beginning to the right (west). Save the Little Prairie Loop for the return trip and continue downward

The Big Prairie at Cooper Mountain

to the right. The path exits the trees and curves south into the open where you're presented with a wide view of the Tualatin River valley; an interpretive sign nearby provides info about some of the area's natural features and wildlife. Veer right (west) through the next two forks, to stay on the Cooper Mountain Loop. Alongside the path, tall shrubs of checker mallow and Oregon grape explode in pink and yellow blooms in early spring.

The path heads back into the trees, where you'll find snowberry, blackberry, trillium, and violets along the trailside. It then crosses a wide bridge over a small creek and comes to another fork at 0.4 mile. Veer left (south) on the Overlook Trail and descend out of the trees to the edge of the prairie and another interpretive sign. Here, enjoy more wide views of the valley and Big Prairie amid groves of moss-draped white oaks. Try using the listening horn for birdsong in the trees. Continue descending the mountain, merging back onto the Cooper Mountain Trail, with woods on your right (west) and the prairie on your left (east). In the spring, the savanna is decorated with a colorful patchwork of pink and blue forget-me-nots, violet blue-eyed Marys and Oregon irises, white rock larkspur, and yellow dandelions. Watch out—there's also plenty of poison oak in the area.

The path loops around the bottom of the hill and begins climbing the opposite side of the savanna, where it turns east and crosses the creek again. Just beyond, take a peek at the quarry pond and try to spot red-legged tree frogs and salamanders. At 1.2 miles, the Larkspur Loop veers to the right (see Go Farther); stay left on the Cooper Mountain Loop to the next junction. Here, the Cooper Mountain Loop veers left (north) for a steady climb back up the hill. Instead, veer right (northeast) on Blacktail Way for a curving ascent under oak and madrone trees. The path crosses another fern-choked creek, then intersects the Little Prairie Loop at 1.7 miles. Turn right (east) for the final portion of the loop. Almost immediately after, take another quick right (east) on a short side trail to the Little Prairie viewpoint. Take a peek for some of the local wildlife, then backtrack to the main trail. Veer right again (north) and ascend through a shady stand of Douglas firs to return to the upper junction, then right (north) one more time to complete your walk.

GO FARTHER

Add the Larkspur Loop to your hike for a little more scenery and wildflower-peeping. Near the bottom of the Cooper Mountain Loop, this 0.7-mile lollipop branches east through a verdant ravine of Douglas fir and sword fern. It dips to cross a bridged creek, then ascends to the loop junction. Veer left (northeast) to make a clockwise circuit around a grove of white oaks sprinkled with more rock larkspur. When you complete the loop, backtrack to the main trail and continue on.

32 Tualatin River National Wildlife Refuge

DISTANCE:	4.5 miles of trails
ELEVATION GAIN:	Up to 70 feet
HIGH POINT:	150 feet
DIFFICULTY:	Easy
FITNESS:	Walkers
FAMILY-FRIENDLY:	Suitable for all ages
DOG-FRIENDLY:	Not permitted
BIKE-FRIENDLY:	Not permitted
AMENITIES:	Parking, wildlife center, interpretive info, restrooms, viewpoints, bird blind (reservations required)
MANAGEMENT:	US Fish and Wildlife Service
GPS:	N 45° 22.932', W 122° 49.890'
OTHER:	Refuge hours sunrise to sunset; wildlife center hours 10:00 AM to 4:00 PM Tuesday–Sunday, closed Monday. The Friends of the Refuge offer youth nature camps, photography workshops, the annual Tualatin River Bird Festival, and a variety of volunteer opportunities to support the refuge. Visit their website for more info.

GETTING THERE

Transit: TriMet buses 93 and 94 make stops right near the refuge entrance.

Driving: From Portland, drive approximately 6 miles south on I-5. Take exit 294 and continue south on State Route 99W for another 7 miles. Turn right into the refuge parking area.

As one of America's only urban wildlife refuges, the Tualatin River natural area is a shining example of how nature rebounds—and thrives—following human encroachment and development. Encompassing more than 1800 acres of Tualatin River floodplain and wetlands, the area has been reclaimed by a vast array of native flora and fauna, including rare

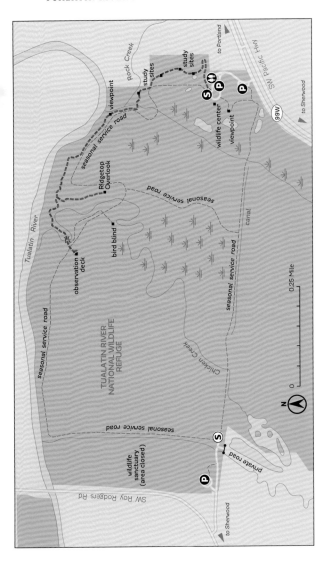

Viewpoint at Tualatin Refuge

wildflowers, small and large mammals, numerous amphibians, and more than two hundred bird species. Visitors are invited to come and observe the area's local residents on two main trails that explore grassy lowlands, seasonal marshes, and verdant forest. This is a fantastic, year-round outdoor destination for locals and visitors, young and old alike. Bring your binoculars!

GET MOVING

Begin your walk at the trailhead near the restroom building, on the north side of the parking area. At the fork, veer right (east) onto the year-round trail and descend into a grove of oak, pine, aspen, and maple trees. The path meanders along, passing several study sites that examine specific natural

TUALATIN REFUGE WILDLIFE GUIDE

The Tualatin River National Wildlife Refuge is home to more than 160 species of nesting and migratory birds, and more than 50 mammals and amphibians. Here is a list of just some of the species you may spot. Pick up a refuge wildlife guide at the wildlife center to take on your walk. Photographers, you can make reservations to use the refuge's bird blind and hope to capture images of some of the winged residents.

BIRDS

- Bittern
- Chickadee
- Cormorant
- Crane
- Dove
- Dowitcher
- Duck
- Egret
- Finch
- Flycatcher
- Goose
- Grebe
- Grosbeak
- Gull
- Heron
- Hummer
- Jay
- Kinglet
- Nuthatch
- Oriole
- Pigeon
- Pipit
- Plover
- Rail
- Sandpiper
- Snipe
- Sparrow
- Spoonbill
- Starling
- Swallow
- Swan
- Swift
- Tern
- Thrush
- Warbler
- Woodpecker
- Wren

RAPTORS

- Eagle
- Falcon
- Harrier
- Hawk
- Kestrel
- Kite
- Osprey
- Owl
- Vulture

MAMMALS

- Bat
- Beaver
- Bobcat
- Coyote
- Deer
- Elk
- Fox
- Gopher
- Mole
- Mouse
- Nutria
- Opossum
- Otter
- Rabbit
- Raccoon
- Skunk
- Squirrel

AMPHIBIANS

- Frog
- Newt
- Salamander

REPTILES

- Lizard
- Snake
- Turtle

features of the area, including vernal ponds, oak savanna, and lush stream banks. Look for pretty pink puffs of red clover, yellow creeping buttercups, and yellow meadow goat's beard lining the trailside.

The trail comes parallel with the seasonal service road and arrives at the river overlook at 0.4 mile. Veer off the trail here to the viewpoint and scan up and down the Tualatin River for frogs, turtles, otters, osprey, and eagles. Return to the walking path and proceed across an open grassy meadow. Watch in areas like this for rabbits, voles, deer, elk, coyotes, and foxes. At 0.5 mile, the trail plunges into cool Douglas fir and cedar forest, where the trailside becomes lined with fern, thimbleberry, duckfoot, and Oregon grape. In this shady environ, look for little pink (invasive) herb Robert, white inside-out flower, and white Columbia windflower.

Around the 0.8-mile mark, take an optional side trip to the Ridgetop Overlook, at the end of a 0.1-mile ascending spur. The view from the top is partially obstructed by trees, but it gives you peeks over the wider wetlands below. The main path continues over Chicken Creek, then exits the forest to a wide junction at 0.9 mile. Cross the seasonal service road and proceed to the large observation deck at the edge of the wetlands. Here is where you start looking for some of the area's many winged residents (see wildlife list). Around the deck are several interpretive signs with information about the wetlands and its inhabitants, as well as several benches for sitting back and watching.

During the fall and winter seasons, retrace your steps back to your starting point. During the spring and summer periods, you can continue exploring the area on the seasonal service road paths (see Go Farther) to make a larger, 3.5-mile loop around the entire area.

GO FARTHER

From the observation deck junction, turn west on the gravel service road and proceed to walk the perimeter of the wetlands area. Be sure to watch the meadows carefully for birds and critters. The path eventually bends south through another grove of trees; here, look for large white field bindweed and clusters of purple forktooth ookow. At the next junction, at 2 miles, turn left (east) and walk alongside a water channel on a slightly raised dike. At 2.5 miles, turn left again (north; continuing east proceeds to the bus stop at the refuge entrance) and cross right through the wetlands area. Look for a variety of waterfowl as well as beavers near the water's edge. At the final junction, turn right and parallel the year-round trail for 0.7 mile back to the parking area and wildlife center.

Next page: *There's plenty of room to roam around the Columbia and Sandy Rivers (Hike 35).*

TROUTDALE

About ten miles east of the Portland metro area, the small town of Troutdale rests near the mouth of the Sandy River, at the western gateway to the Columbia River Gorge National Scenic Area. This small, unassuming town—an easy, twenty-minute drive from Portland's metro area—features several parks and natural areas that offer a variety of walking paths and easy hiking trails ideal for stretching your legs or taking your pup for a stroll. With most of these locations situated near forest, wetlands, or riversides, many of them also offer exceptional wildlife- and bird-watching throughout the spring, summer, and fall seasons. Pack a picnic and your binoculars, and spend a morning, afternoon, or entire day at any one of these areas.

33 **Blue Lake Regional Park**

DISTANCE:	3 miles of paths and trails
ELEVATION GAIN:	None
HIGH POINT:	28 feet
DIFFICULTY:	Easy
FITNESS:	Walkers, runners, cyclists, some barrier-free
FAMILY-FRIENDLY:	Suitable for all ages; children under five not permitted in lake
DOG-FRIENDLY:	Not permitted
BIKE-FRIENDLY:	Paved paths only
AMENITIES:	Parking, restrooms, picnic areas, boat rentals, sports fields, discovery garden, fishing, swimming
MANAGEMENT:	Oregon Metro
GPS:	N 45° 33.312', W 122° 26.802'
OTHER:	Park hours 8:00 AM to sunset; vehicle fee

GETTING THERE

Transit: Not available.

Driving: From Portland, drive east on I-84 to Troutdale. Take exit 17, turn left onto NE Marine Drive, and proceed for 2.7 miles to NE Blue Lake Road. Turn left and continue 0.3 mile to the park entrance on the right. Proceed through the pay station and turn left into the parking area.

Bike: From the I-205 Trail at the Glenn Jackson Bridge, ride 4.6 miles east on the 40-Mile Loop trail (NE Marine Drive) to the park's western entrance; from the Troutdale area, ride approximately 3 miles west on the 40-Mile Loop trail (NE Marine Drive) to the park's main entrance.

Blue Lake Park is a pleasant summer destination for picnics, paddleboating, and disc golf, with several paved paths that wind throughout the park and along the banks of pretty Blue Lake. The park also features a discovery garden where visitors

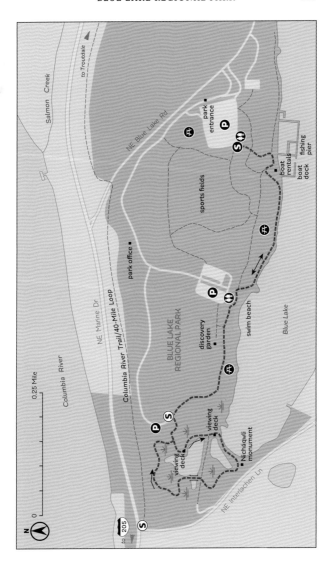

Blue Lake, from the Nicháqwli monument

of all ages can learn about Northwest flora and fauna. At the west end of the lake, a series of gravel trails wind through a wetlands area of lily ponds and mixed forest to a Native American cultural site with views of Larch Mountain and distant Mount Hood. Pack a picnic, bring a Frisbee, and plan to spend the day lounging under tall shade trees after you've taken your walk.

GET MOVING

Walking the entire length of the park and back—a 1.75-mile roundtrip—can be done in about an hour. But with several things to see along the way, give yourself a little extra time. From the main parking area, walk on a paved path to the boat dock area. Turn right (west) and proceed along the lakeshore, where snowberry lines portions of the trail, and several picnic areas can be found under big-leaf maples. Squirrels dart here and there collecting nuts and seeds, while a variety of birds chirp and sing in the trees overhead. Look for bald eagles and ospreys; the latter are common here.

After just 0.3 mile, the path circuits around the swim beach area and a large restroom building. Shortly beyond, the park's discovery garden is located on the right. Take a detour into the garden, where you can see a variety of interpretive displays with information about the park's native plants and animals. There's special see, touch, and smell displays for young explorers. Head back to the paved path and continue along; the route turns away from the lake and proceeds under big trees. At just over a half mile, shortly after the path bends north, a gravel trail branches off to the left (west).

Turn left onto the wetlands trail and cross a grassy meadow; veer left where the trail forks to begin a clockwise circuit around the wetland area. Pause at the viewing deck at the edge of a large lily pond and begin your search for the park's resident ducks, beavers, otters, and frogs. Moving on, continue straight (south) through a junction and proceed along the lakeshore, with another lily pond on the right. Near the marshy foot of the lake, where the path turns again, a small monument of totems and carved canoes pays tribute to the Chinook Nicháqwli village that used to occupy these lands. The view across the lake and of distant mountains is splendid.

The path loops through mixed woodland to another four-way junction; continue straight (north) through this one also and cross a bridge over the back side of the large lily pond you saw earlier; check again for any local residents. The path snakes through trees for a short spell, then heads back out into the open and reconnects with the wetlands path. Turn left (east) and retrace your steps back through the park to your starting point.

34 Sandy River Delta

DISTANCE:	9.3 miles of trails
ELEVATION GAIN:	Up to 120 feet
HIGH POINT:	50 feet
DIFFICULTY:	Easy
FITNESS:	Walkers, hikers, runners, cyclists, equestrians
FAMILY-FRIENDLY:	Suitable for all ages; *a lot* of dogs; some open shoreline
DOG-FRIENDLY:	Permitted; leashed in parking area and on Confluence Trail
BIKE-FRIENDLY:	Permitted
AMENITIES:	Parking, restrooms, picnic tables
MANAGEMENT:	US Forest Service, Columbia River Gorge
GPS:	N 45° 32.760', W 122° 22.428'
OTHER:	Park hours 6:00 AM to 8:00 PM in spring and fall; 6:00 AM to 10:00 PM in summer; 6:00 AM to 6:00 PM in winter. In winter and spring, it's not uncommon for low-lying portions of the park to flood.

GETTING THERE

Transit: Not available.

Driving: From I-205 in East Portland, merge onto I-84 east and drive 9.7 miles, through Troutdale. Take exit 18 for Oxbow Regional Park and turn right (north) at the bottom of the ramp. Follow the road around to the right (east) for 0.3 mile; enter the park and proceed to the parking area and trailheads.

Bike: Ride the 40-Mile Loop trail to Troutdale. Proceed through town and cross the Sandy River on the Historic Columbia River Highway. Turn left (northwest) on NE Jordan Road and continue 0.9 mile to the park entrance.

East of Portland, at the gates of the Columbia River Gorge National Scenic Area, the Sandy River Delta is a broad wetland near the convergence of the Sandy and Columbia

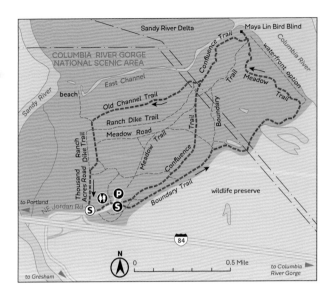

Rivers. Here, among grassy meadows, colorful wildflowers, and stands of willow, ash, cottonwood, and dogwood, more than 9 miles of trails invite walkers, runners, hikers, equestrians, and mountain bikers to mix and match trail sections to enjoy riverfront outings, from quick trail fixes to longer explorations. And as Portland's largest off-leash dog-walking area, you're welcome to bring along your four-legged friend.

GET MOVING

For a short and easy outing that lets you enjoy both sunny meadows and cool woodland, walk the Confluence Trail to the Maya Lin Bird Blind. This 2.6-mile out-and-back starts from the upper parking area and proceeds northeast, with rustling woodland to the left (north) and open grassland to the right (south). Along the fringes of the trail, look for red clover, European centaury, and arumleaf arrowhead. Near 0.6 mile, in the middle of a wide-open clearing, the trail bends north and

Explore the banks of the Columbia at Sandy Delta.

proceeds through a four-way junction. As you near a series of powerlines, the trail forks three ways; choose the middle fork, bending northeast, and proceed into shady woods. Continue under the trees on a snowberry-lined path, where you'll begin to spy the Sandy's east channel through the trees. Near 1.3 miles, fork left (north) at a junction and proceed just a few more paces to the blind. Inside the cage-like structure, the names of many of the plants and animals Lewis and Clark recorded on their journey are listed on the blind's slats. How many did you observe on your stroll there? Return by the same route, or mix it up with one of the other trails on your way back.

For a longer outing that circuits the entire delta area, combine the Boundary, Meadow, Confluence, and Old Channel Trails for a 3.4-mile loop. Start on the Boundary Trail, an old roadbed that skirts the edge of the park area along a split-rail fence. On bluebird days, you'll be able to easily pick out Larch Mountain in the near distance. Look for colorful summer blooms of penstemon and common tansy along the trailside, in addition to large invasive blackberry shrubs. At a wide four-way junction at 0.8 mile, veer right (east) onto the Meadow Trail to continue along the edge of the park area. A posted sign indicates a wildlife area closed to the public; scan here for critters roaming in the meadows. The path proceeds through a stretch of overgrown reed canary grass to an unmarked fork. If river levels are low (summer, fall), you can proceed to the right (northeast) through a narrow cluster of trees to the riverside and walk the riverbank all the way to the East Channel confluence and the Maya Lin Bird Blind. If river levels are high (winter, spring), turn left (northwest) and continue along the Meadow Trail.

From the fork, the Meadow Trail meanders through small meadows and groves of cottonwood to another junction at 1.9 miles. Take the right fork for a quick visit to the Maya Lin Bird Blind, then backtrack and turn right (west) onto the Confluence Trail; proceed through the shady woods brimming with blackberry, snowberry, and Pacific ninebark to a wide junction under crackling powerlines. Turn right (northwest) to go between two powerline towers, then make a quick left (southwest) onto the Old Channel Trail. The trail continues

DELTA WILDLIFE

Regardless of which trails you wander around the Sandy River Delta, keep your eyes peeled for mule deer, coyotes, bobcats, raccoons, skunks, and some of the more than sixty species of birds that inhabit the area. Bring your binocs and search for kestrels, swallows, juncos, woodpeckers, warblers, wrens, hawks, eagles, and osprey. If you wander down to the riverside, also look for river otters, turtles, a variety of waterfowl, herons, and kingfishers, as well as dragonflies and red-legged frogs.

through more open grassland, then ducks back under shady cottonwoods and dogwoods; watch for creeping blackberry trying to snag your socks and pants. At 2.9 miles, the path comes to a wide T-junction with Thousand Acres Road. (You can follow the road right [north] to a sandy beach; beyond that is a maze of unmapped, unmarked user paths.) Turn left (south) on the road and follow it through a shallow, open basin with peeks of Mount Hood, then along an old dike under more trees to its end at the park road. Turn left (east) one more time and return to the main parking lot.

BIKE IT

All of the paths in the Sandy River Delta park are open to mountain bikes, allowing you to connect trails at will for countless combinations of loops, figure eights, and other options. The only challenge is that this popular park is often crowded with dog walkers, trail runners, and, on summer weekends, a lot of families with children. Exercise good trail manners, ride with caution around the crowds, and give right-of-way to equestrians by pulling to the side and allowing them to pass.

35 Oxbow Regional Park

DISTANCE:	12 miles of trails
ELEVATION GAIN:	Up to 510 feet
HIGH POINT:	700 feet
DIFFICULTY:	Easy to moderate
FITNESS:	Walkers, hikers, runners, cyclists, equestrians
FAMILY-FRIENDLY:	Suitable for all ages; some steep trails, open shoreline; beware of poison oak
DOG-FRIENDLY:	Not permitted
BIKE-FRIENDLY:	Paved roads and some trails
AMENITIES:	Parking, restrooms, picnic areas, interpretive info, camping, fishing, swimming

MANAGEMENT:	Oregon Metro
GPS:	N 45° 29.826', W 122° 17.418'
OTHER:	Park hours 6:30 AM to sunset; vehicle fee

GETTING THERE

Transit: Not available.

Driving: From Southeast Portland, drive SE Division Street east for approximately 10 miles (from I-205); continue on SE Division Drive for another 1.4 miles. Veer right on SE Oxbow Drive for 2.2 miles, then left on SE Hosner Road for 1.4 miles. Follow the road right into Oxbow Regional Park and drive the park road to its end for trailheads and camping.

Located just thirty minutes east of Portland's metro area, Oxbow Regional Park comprises one thousand acres of forested canyon ridges and rocky beaches situated on the banks of the Wild and Scenic Sandy River, just a few miles upstream from where it empties into the mighty

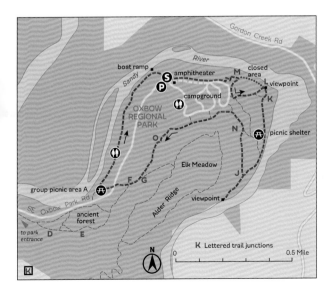

Columbia River. Here, the river makes three dramatic wide bends (referred to as oxbow bends, hence the park's moniker) as it continues to wear away at the loose rock and sand deposited by lahars that sloughed off Mount Hood centuries ago. Today, we can enjoy it as one of the Portland area's wildest river parks.

With more than 12 miles of trails in the park, it can take you multiple visits to hike them all—or one long day. The advantage to hiking a smaller portion is that it gives you the opportunity for multiple visits to a park that is definitely worth returning to. Here, you can choose between riverside walks, forest romps, and wooded meadow strolls among small and large loops all interconnected with a park-length path. As you're walking, be alert for the abundance of wildlife known to inhabit the waters, land, and trees in the canyon. This includes

Wander river and forest on the Sandy River at Oxbow Regional Park.

RIVERBANK EROSION

Oxbow Regional Park is a very dynamic landscape in that the Sandy River is constantly wearing away at the soft sediment banks on its riversides. Because water is persistent and always looks for the most direct way downhill, these oxbows will eventually disappear, and the river will form a straighter channel through the area. You can see this process in action by observing the collapsed banks along some portions of the riverside trail. In several areas, the bluff has sloughed off. Trees and shrubs have fallen into the river, and trails have disappeared. Park staff and volunteers continually work to keep trails open and safe for hikers, but occasionally you may see portions of trail closed as detours and repairs become necessary.

steelhead, salmon, otters, beavers, raccoons, deer, elk, black bears, woodpeckers, owls, osprey, and eagles—just to name a few.

GET MOVING

The best hiking introduction to Oxbow Regional Park is a 2.6-mile horseshoe loop trail at the upper end of the park. The outer leg of the trail follows the banks of the Sandy, while the inner leg passes through ancient forest, where moss drapes from firs, cedars, and maples; summer wildflowers bloom; little critters dart here and there; and birds chirp and sing overhead. In autumn, these same paths become quiet and colorful, as the air chills and the crowds dissipate, and big-leaf maple leaves carpet the trails. Start at the trailhead at the end of the park road and walk east along the river, past the amphitheater and campground, where you're presented with views over the river. Interpretive signs along the way describe the dynamic habits of riverfront erosion.

The route then drops through a few switchbacks into fern- and salal-carpeted forest and comes to a junction marked "M" at 0.3 mile. Here, a couple of well-worn user

Sunlight streams through a canopy of vine maple.

paths proceed left (north) to the river. This is one of the best spots for accessing the rocky riverside, so explore at will. The trail forward from this junction has been closed (see sidebar), so turn right (south) to continue. At the next junction, at 0.4 mile, the path right (west) proceeds to climb steeply to the campground, and the path straight ahead continues through the trees. Instead of these, turn left (east) and proceed back toward the river, forking left at a junction along the way. Once you reach the river at a junction marked "L," you'll have another nice look at the Wild and Scenic Sandy. In fall, watch for spawning Chinook salmon in the river's riffles. Turn right (south) and follow the river upstream, keeping your eyes peeled for wildlife. Fork left through an unmarked junction and proceed to a large clearing with a group picnic shelter at 0.8 mile.

Continue south, keeping the river on your left until you reach a junction marked "J" at 1 mile. For a little more exploring, continue straight (south) for about a quarter mile to a sandy embankment with nice river views. To continue the loop, turn right (north) into the forest and begin a gentle ascent to circuit the base of Alder Ridge. Proceed to a junction marked "N" and veer left (northwest) onto a wide, gravel path. (Right [east] returns to the picnic shelter.) The path proceeds to skirt the south side of the campground, then climbs to meet a gravel road at 1.8 miles. (You can add the 1.8-mile Elk Meadow loop by turning left here; see Go Farther.) Veer right and descend the gravel road to the paved park road. Cross the park road and proceed across an open lawn to the riverside trail; turn right and continue along the river to the boat ramp at 2.5 miles. Turn right (southeast) and walk up the ramp to the parking area where you started.

GO FARTHER

For more mileage, and perhaps a view of the area's resident elk herd, add the 1.8-mile Elk Meadow loop to your outing. From either the horseshoe loop above, or the park road near picnic area A, make a steady ascent up an old logging road to the top of Alder Ridge. When you reach the junction, you can hike the loop in either direction. The trail remains in the trees around the top of the plateau, but there are several views of the meadow on the interior as you make your way around. This is a popular equestrian route, so if you happen across some riders, be sure to give them the proper courtesy and step aside to let them pass. Once you've completed the full circuit, descend the old road again and continue your journey.

Next page: *Circuit the city on the 40-Mile Loop and enjoy the many parks and urban forests along the way (Hike 36).*

PORTLAND 40-MILE LOOP

Parks should be connected . . . and improved to take advantage of beautiful natural scenery . . . [to] form an admirable park system for such an important city as Portland is bound to become. —John Olmsted

The concept of a bike and pedestrian path circling the entire Portland regional area is more than a century old. It began in 1904 as part of the Olmsted Brothers' efforts to beautify Portland and establish a citywide parks system. This was very progressive thinking, considering that at the time the Portland area was still mostly open prairies and wooded hillsides. The original 40-Mile Loop was intended to link many of these proposed parks together as a way to provide easy means for the public to access them. However, as Portland grew over the decades, so did the loop, as it now creates a grand circuit around Portland, Gresham, and Troutdale, and traces the banks of the Columbia, Willamette, and Sandy Rivers, as well as Johnson Creek.

More than a century later, the 40-Mile Loop—now more than 140 miles—is still a work in progress. Construction on the trail really took off in the 1980s, and efforts continue to move forward to complete the few final gaps and see this grand trail vision come to final fruition. Despite its unfinished state, walkers, runners, and cyclists can still enjoy long portions of the trail in most areas with minimal off-trail inconvenience, thanks to recommended detours provided by the 40-Mile Land Trust. Even more, the loop can be used to access many of the trails included in this guide, giving outdoor enthusiasts the option to ride or walk to nearby parks instead of drive. Additionally, the 40-Mile Loop offers a few treasures of its own worth exploring.

40-MILE LOOP ACCESS

You can access the 40-Mile Loop at the following locations, counter-clockwise from downtown Portland. Some areas have parking available, others can be accessed via public transit. (See the full trail map on the following pages.)

Downtown:
A Tom McCall Waterfront Park
B Eastbank Esplanade, near OMSI
C Springwater trailhead at SE Ivon Street and SE 4th Avenue

Sellwood:
D SE Spokane Street and SE Oaks Park Drive
E Springwater trailhead at SE Ochoco Street and SE 19th Avenue

Errol Heights:
F Springwater crossing at SE Johnson Creek Boulevard, south of SE 45th Avenue

Lents:
G Springwater crossing at SE 82nd Avenue, south of SE Foster Road
H Springwater crossing at SE Foster Road, east of SE 103rd Avenue

Powellhurst:
I Springwater crossing at SE 122nd Avenue, south of SE Harold Street
J South side of Powell Butte Nature Park

Gresham:
K Main City Park at Gresham Butte

Walk, run, or ride on Portland's 40-Mile Trail.

Troutdale:

   L   NE Marine Drive near Blue Lake Park

Columbia River:

   M   NE Marine Drive at I-205 Trail

   N   NE Marine Drive at Broughton Beach Park, east of
           NE 33rd Avenue

North Portland:

   O   Trailhead at Smith and Bybee Lakes

   P   Trailhead at N. Marine Drive and NE Lombard Street,
           near Kelley Point Park

St. Johns:

   Q   NE Lombard Street at N. Philadelphia Avenue

Forest Park:

   R   Hikers: Wildwood Trail at NW Germantown Road (west)

   S   Hikers: Wildwood and Marquam Trails at Washington
           Park (east)

   T   Bikes: Leif Erikson Drive at NW Springville Road (west)

   U   Bikes: Leif Erikson Drive at NW Aspen Avenue (east)

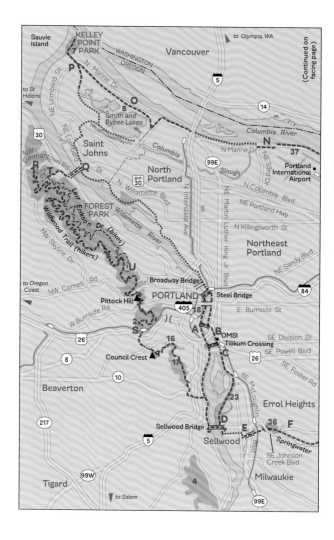

(Continued on facing page)

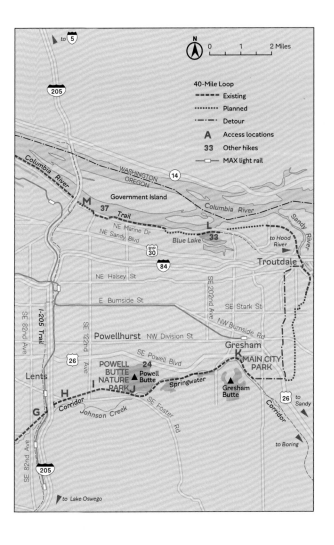

36 Springwater Corridor and Tideman Johnson Park

DISTANCE:	3 miles roundtrip
ELEVATION GAIN:	200 feet
HIGH POINT:	110 feet
DIFFICULTY:	Easy to moderate
FITNESS:	Walkers, runners, cyclists, barrier-free
FAMILY-FRIENDLY:	Suitable for all ages; moderate bike traffic
DOG-FRIENDLY:	Leashed
BIKE-FRIENDLY:	Permitted
AMENITIES:	Parking, picnic areas, interpretive info, creek views
MANAGEMENT:	Oregon Metro
GPS:	N 45° 27.522', W 122° 38.706'
OTHER:	As of 2018, the Springwater Corridor is incomplete between SE Umatilla Street and the trailhead at SE Ochoco Street and SE 19th Avenue

GETTING THERE

Transit: TriMet bus 70 makes stops at the corner of SE 17th Street and SE Ochoco Street. Walk two blocks east to the Springwater trailhead.

Driving: From SE Tacoma Street in Sellwood, drive south on SE 19th Street to the end of the road at SE Linn Street. Find street parking near the corner, then walk the paved path south to the trailhead at SE Ochoco Street.

Bike: Ride the Springwater Corridor from either direction; see Bike It.

One of the most enjoyable segments of the 40-Mile Loop is the Springwater Corridor, a 21-mile section of paved path that reaches from the Willamette River, near Tilikum Crossing, all the way to the town of Boring. One of the most scenic sections is along Johnson Creek, which includes a stretch

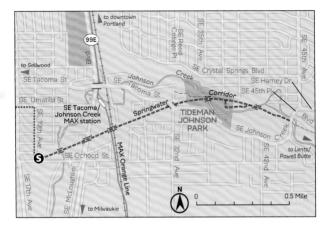

through Tideman Johnson Park, a seven-acre pocket of riparian wilderness in a narrow wooded gorge. Though small, the area possesses a rich diversity of wildlife that makes the canyon and creek side their home. Common residents include owls, herons, woodpeckers, grosbeaks, beavers, and coyotes. There's also a variety of fish in the creek, including salmon and steelhead.

GET MOVING

For a nice stroll along the Springwater Corridor through Tideman Johnson Park, start at the trailhead at SE Ochoco Street and SE 19th Avenue in Sellwood. Get on the trail and start walking east. The first part of the path proceeds over a series of bridges that cross Johnson Creek, SE McLoughlin Boulevard, and a series of railroad tracks. The views of the city and industrial areas are uninspiring, but the bridges are fun to cross. Once you're over the bridges, at 0.6 mile, the route becomes more pleasant in a corridor of maples and alders, with pink sweet pea and purple chicory adorning the trailside.

The path ascends at a barely perceptible grade, but the slopes on either side suddenly vault high above, putting you in a lush ravine. In springtime, the slopes often "weep" with water seeping out of the hillsides and across the path. At about the 1-mile mark, the trail crosses Johnson Creek again. Just beyond, a side trail branches right (south) to descend into the riparian area in Tideman Johnson Park. Take this 0.2-mile side loop under verdant tree cover and amid large shrubs of orange jewelweed and yellow primrose. The side trail reconnects with the Springwater Corridor near a large viewing deck above Johnson Creek. Continue east on the Springwater path to complete your trip through the canyon. When you reach the trailhead at SE Johnson Creek Boulevard, do an about-face and return the way you came.

GO FARTHER

Of course, the trail doesn't stop at SE Johnson Creek Boulevard. You can keep going all the way to Powell Butte and beyond. However, the next several miles proceed alongside the road through an industrial area and a segment that is often populated with homeless camps. If you want to do more, make your way through Sellwood and pick up the Springwater

Canada thistle along Johnson Creek

Corridor again near Sellwood Riverfront Park. Here you can access the Oaks Bottom Wildlife Refuge (Hike 23). You can do the loop around the wetlands in either direction, then head into downtown Sellwood for coffee and antique shopping.

BIKE IT

If you're cycling and would like to visit Tideman Johnson Park, get some extra mileage by starting at the Springwater trail-head on SE Ivon Street, near Tilikum Crossing. Begin with a pleasant 3-mile cruise south alongside the Willamette River, passing Ross Island and proceeding through the Oaks Bottom Wildlife Refuge (Hike 23) to Sellwood. Turn left (east) off the Springwater route onto SE Umatilla Street and ride 0.7 mile to SE 19th Avenue; turn right (south) and roll 0.3 mile down to the Springwater trailhead and continue as indicated above.

37 Columbia River Trail

DISTANCE:	11 miles of paths
ELEVATION GAIN:	Up to 90 feet
HIGH POINT:	50 feet
DIFFICULTY:	Easy
FITNESS:	Walkers, runners, cyclists, barrier-free
FAMILY-FRIENDLY:	Suitable for all ages; moderate auto, bike traffic
DOG-FRIENDLY:	Leashed
BIKE-FRIENDLY:	Permitted
AMENITIES:	Paved path, views
MANAGEMENT:	Oregon Metro
GPS:	N 45° 34.380', W 122° 32.748'
OTHER:	Portions of this route may be on sidewalk or the road

GETTING THERE

Transit: Ride the MAX Red Line north to the Portland Airport; depart at the Cascades Station. Walk 0.2 mile south on NE

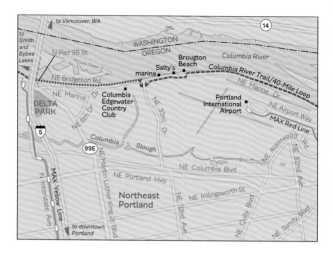

Mount St. Helens Avenue, then east on NE Alderwood Road for 0.3 mile. Turn left (north) on the I-205 Trail and walk 0.6 mile to the 40-Mile Loop at NE Marine Drive.

Driving: From Southeast Portland, drive I-205 north toward Washington State. Take exit 24B for NE Airport Way East, and merge onto Airport Way for 0.7 mile. At NE 122nd Avenue, turn left and proceed just 0.2 mile to NE Marine Drive. Turn left again and go 0.8 mile to where the I-205 Trail meets the 40-Mile Loop. Find street parking nearby.

Bike: Ride the I-205 Trail north from anywhere in East Portland; 11 miles from Clackamas Town Center.

For great views of the Columbia River, Government Island, and Mount Hood, you can stroll or ride along the northern portion of the 40-Mile Loop. The wide paved path parallels Marine Drive for 20 miles, from Kelley Point Park (Hike 7) to the west all the way to Troutdale to the east. The most scenic stretch of path is from I-205 to Blue Lake Park (Hike 33). Traveling alongside the Columbia offers great opportunities for bird- and wildlife-watching. Eagles, osprey, and herons are

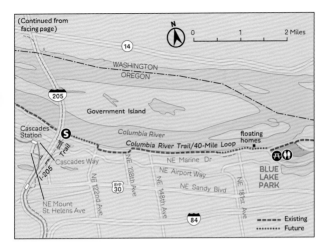

commonly seen; occasionally, sea lions may be spotted in the river hunting for fish. Sunrises and sunsets can also be pretty spectacular from right alongside the river.

GET MOVING

For walking or riding the Columbia River portion of the 40-Mile Loop, start on NE Marine Drive near the I-205 bridge and head east. The way proceeds along the roadside or on a level path next to the road; occasionally it dips toward the river, below the road level, then back up, and continues on. As you cruise along, sailboats and barges may be seen plying the river; birds of prey might be perched on the boughs of trees on Government Island, just across the water. There will also likely be plenty of giant steel birds (airplanes) screaming overhead as they come in for landing at Portland International Airport.

The way is pretty straightforward, as in there's only one way to go. Along the way, the land side of the route is mostly the backsides of industrial complexes, so it's much nicer to keep your attention on the river and mountains ahead. On

Sunrise on the Columbia River

clear days, the broad peak to the east that appears to have a notch cut out of its summit is Larch Mountain; Mount Hood can often be seen in the farther distance. Around 3.5 miles out, the path passes several clusters of floating homes on the Columbia, between the mainland and a smaller wooded island. Shortly past the floating community, at 4.8 miles, cross Marine Drive into Blue Lake Regional Park (Hike 33). Here, you can wander the park's paths, have a picnic, toss a Frisbee, or just take a nap under a tall, shady tree. When you're ready, return by the same route.

GO FARTHER

Want more? You can add up to another 24 miles (roundtrip) by walking, skating, running, or riding the river path from I-205 westward. Start at the same place and just head west. The path is similar, mostly flat and along a slightly raised berm, sidewalks, and roadside bike paths. For nearly 5 miles, the path traces the northern boundary of Portland International Airport, so all the views are over the river. Just before leaving the airport behind, at 4.5 miles, the trail passes Salty's on the Columbia River, a nice place to enjoy happy hour après and river views.

Moving on, the path passes the Columbia Edgewater Country Club, then proceeds along a narrow channel on the Columbia packed with boat docks, garages, and floating homes. At about 7 miles, near I-5, the trail runs out and turns into surface streets. This makes a good turnaround point. If you want to go farther still, use N. Pier 99 Street to access N. Marine Drive on the west side of the highway. From this point, you can reach the Smith and Bybee Wetlands (Hike 8) in another 2.1 miles and Kelley Point Park (Hike 7) in another 4.5 miles.

ACKNOWLEDGMENTS

BEFORE STARTING THIS GUIDEBOOK PROJECT, I had already walked, hiked, and pedaled many of the locations listed in this guide. As I revisited these locations and explored many new ones in my research for this book, I was reminded of why Portland is such a special place to live. The Portland area's urban park system is second to none. No matter where you live in the city, there is a park, preserve, or urban forest usually within just a few minutes' drive, walk, bus, or bike ride. So thanks, Portland—you're awesome!

I would also like to thank Kate Rogers and Mountaineers Books for the opportunity to continue working together, and allowing me to showcase this selection of trails for everyone living in—or visiting—Portland and the surrounding communities. Thanks also to Dario, Julie, Bonnie, and the wonderful crew at Marino Adriatic Café for continuing to indulge me in using their establishment as my de facto book-writing work space, where the coffee (best cappuccino in Portland!), the music, and the camaraderie are all delightful.

And last but not least, thanks to my incredible wife, Mitzi, who continues to support this book-writing habit of mine, who makes a great hiking partner and photo model, and who helps me keep my head on straight through the roller coaster of excitement, exasperation, and exhaustion that goes hand in hand with researching and writing these things. You're the best, babe! The best!

Opposite: *Sunrise view from Mount Tabor* (Photo by Mitzi Sugar)

GUIDE TO COMMON WILDFLOWERS, TREES, AND SHRUBS

PART OF THE JOY OF HIKING in Portland's parks and urban forests are the many varieties of trees, shrubs, and flowering plants growing there. The following pages contain a visual guide for some of the most common ones you're likely to see on your outings around Portland. Summer is the prime time for wildflowers; however, some flowers, like trilliums and violets, are common in spring, while buttercups and herb Roberts can be seen through most seasons. Once you get acquainted with the regulars, consider picking up a detailed tree or wildflower guide to help you discover even more.

Opposite: *Sunlight filters through the trees in Forest Park (Hike 11).*

COMMON WILDFLOWERS

1. Bellflower
2. Blue-eyed Mary
3. Broadiaea
4. Buttercup
5. Chicory
6. Columbia windflower
7. Daisy
8. Field bindweed
9. Goats beard
10. Hardhack
11. Hedge nettle
12. Herb Robert

13. Honeysuckle
14. Jewelweed
15. Lupine
16. Nootka rose
17. Ookow
18. Queen Anne's lace
19. Red clover
20. Red currant
21. Thistle
22. Trillium
23. Wild pea
24. Wood violet

COMMON TREES AND SHRUBS

1. Blackberry
2. Duckfoot
3. English ivy
4. Fern, deer
5. Fern, lady
6. Fern, licorice
7. Fern, maidenhair
8. Fern, sword
9. Oregon grape
10. Oregon oxalis
11. Poison oak
12. Salal

13. Salmonberry
14. Thimbleberry
15. Vanilla leaf
16. Big-leaf maple
17. Douglas fir
18. Hemlock
19. Madrone
20. Ponderosa pine
21. Sequoia
22. Vine maple
23. Western red cedar
24. White oak

APPENDIX

TRAIL AND PARK MANAGEMENT

Audubon Society of Portland
(503) 292-6855
http://audubonportland.org

Hillsboro Parks and Recreation
(503) 681-6120
www.hillsboro-oregon.gov/departments/parks-recreation

Hoyt Arboretum
(503) 865-8733
www.hoytarboretum.org

Lake Oswego Parks and Recreation
(503) 675-2549
www.ci.oswego.or.us/parksrec

Oregon Department of Fish and Wildlife
(503) 947-6000
www.dfw.state.or.us

Oregon Metro
(503) 797-1700
www.oregonmetro.gov

Oregon State Parks
(800) 551-6949
http://oregonstateparks.org

Portland Parks and Recreation
(503) 823-7529
www.portlandoregon.gov/parks

Tualatin Hills Parks and Recreation
(503) 645-6433
www.thprd.org

US Fish and Wildlife Service
(503) 625-5944
www.fws.gov

US Forest Service
Columbia River Gorge
(541) 308-1700
www.fs.usda.gov/crgnsa

West Linn Parks and Recreation
(503) 557-4700
http://westlinnoregon.gov/parksrec

TRAIL SUPPORT, CONSERVATION, AND EDUCATION

Cooper Mountain Nature House
(503) 629-6350
www.thprd.org/facilities/nature/cooper-mountain-nature-house

Forest Park Conservancy
(503) 223-5449
www.forestparkconservancy.org

Friends of Lone Fir Cemetery
(503) 224-9200
www.friendsoflonefircemetery.org

Friends of Marquam Nature Park
(971) 599-3667, www.fmnp.org

Friends of Mount Tabor Park
(503) 512-0816
www.taborfriends.org

Friends of the Sandy River Delta
http://fsrd.org

Friends of Springbrook Park
(503) 860-8665
www.springbrookpark.org

Friends of Tideman Johnson Park
www.ardenwald.org/committees/fotjp

Friends of Tryon Creek
www.tryonfriends.org

Friends of Tualatin River National Wildlife Refuge
(503) 625-5944 ex. 227
http://friendsoftualatinrefuge.org

Sauvie Island Community Association
http://sauvieisland.org

Trailkeepers of Oregon
(971) 206-4351
www.trailkeepersoforegon.org

Tualatin Hills Nature Center
(503) 629-6350
www.thprd.org/facilities/nature/nature-center

40-Mile Loop Land Trust
http://40mileloop.org/wordpress/

INDEX

ABOUT THE AUTHOR

ELI BOSCHETTO grew up hiking the high passes and alpine meadows of California's Sierra Nevada before migrating to the Northwest in 2005. Since then, he has extensively hiked, written about, and photographed trails around Oregon, Washington, and British Columbia. Over the  course of his trail journeys, he has performed as a Northwest correspondent for *Backpacker* and served as the editor of *Washington Trails*. Most recently, Eli is the author of *Hiking the Pacific Crest Trail: Oregon* and the founder and director of PCT: Oregon.

When not on the trail or assisting Oregon's PCT hikers, Eli enjoys Portland's local, sustainable food scene, catching the latest flicks at his local theater pub, and building Lego models. Eli lives in Southeast Portland with his wife, Mitzi. You can connect with him online at www.pctoregon.com, or on Facebook and Instagram at @pctoregon.

MOUNTAINEERS BOOKS, including its two imprints, Skipstone and Braided River, is a leading publisher of quality outdoor recreation, sustainability, and conservation titles. As a 501(c)(3) nonprofit, we are committed to supporting the environmental and educational goals of our organization by providing expert information on human-powered adventure, sustainable practices at home and on the trail, and preservation of wilderness.

Our publications are made possible through the generosity of donors, and through sales of more than 800 titles on outdoor recreation, sustainable lifestyle, and conservation. To donate, purchase books, or learn more, visit us online:

MOUNTAINEERS BOOKS

1001 SW Klickitat Way, Suite 201 • Seattle, WA 98134
800-553-4453 • mbooks@mountaineersbooks.org
www.mountaineersbooks.org

Leave No Trace strives to educate visitors about the nature of their recreational impacts and offers techniques to prevent and minimize such impacts. Leave No Trace is best understood as an educational and ethical program, not as a set of rules and regulations. For more information, visit www.lnt.org or call 800-332-4100.

OTHER TITLES YOU MIGHT ENJOY FROM MOUNTAINEERS BOOKS

Best Hikes with Kids: Oregon
2nd Edition
Bonnie Henderson and Zach Urness

Best Hikes with Dogs: Oregon
2nd Edition
Ellen Bishop

Hiking the Pacific Crest Trail: Oregon
Section Hiking from Donomore Pass
to Bridge of the Gods
Eli Boschetto

Biking Portland
55 Rides from the Willamette
Valley to Vancouver
Owen Wozniak

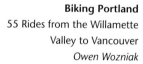

www.mountaineersbooks.org